VULTURES & BUTTER-FLIES

Living the Contradictions

Susan Classen

Herald Press
Scottdale, Pennsylvania
Waterloo, Ontario

Library of Congress Cataloging-in-Publication Data
Classen, Susan, 1957-
    Vultures and butterflies : living the contradictions / Susan
Classen.
      p. cm.
    Includes bibliographical references.
    ISBN 0-8361-3607-1
    1. Classen, Susan, 1957- . 2. Mennonites—Biography.
3. Nurses—El Salvador—Biography. 4. Nurses—Bolivia—
Biography. 5. Persecution—El Salvador. 6. El Salvador—
Politics and government—1979- I. Title.
    BX8143.C56A3 1992
    289.7′092—dc20
    [B]   92-16148
                                            CIP

The paper used in this publication is recycled and meets the minimum requirements of American National Standard for Information Sciences—Permanence of Paper for Printed Library Materials,
ANSI Z39.48-1984.

Scripture quotations are from the *Holy Bible: New International
Version.* Copyright © 1973, 1978, 1984 International Bible Society.
Used by permission of Zondervan Bible Publishers.

VULTURES AND BUTTERFLIES
Copyright © 1992 by Herald Press, Scottdale, Pa. 15683
    Published simultaneously in Canada by Herald Press,
    Waterloo, Ont. N2L 6H7. All rights reserved
Library of Congress Catalog Number: 92-16148
International Standard Book Number: 0-8361-3607-1
Printed in the United States of America
Book design by Gwen M. Stamm
Cover art by Taller Santa Teresa, Comunidad 22 de Abril, San
    Salvador, El Salvador

1 2 3 4 5 6 7 8 9 10 98 97 96 95 94 93 92

To my parents,
who taught me about letting go
through the way
they lived and died.

Contents

Author's Preface

This book was born of contradictions. It is the positive result of my struggle with powerlessness and grief.

In 1989, I agreed to spend two months in North America sharing about my experiences in El Salvador. I had completed one month of the speaking tour when I realized I didn't have the physical or emotional reserves to continue. The day after I broke my speaking commitment, I received a phone call saying that my father had a brain tumor and his prognosis was poor. I went home to Ohio to be with him.

During the next few months I felt guilty and frustrated. I felt guilty that I had stopped speaking at a time when political events made the Salvadoran story particularly crucial. I felt frustrated that I could do nothing for my father besides accompany him as he died. I had to do something.

So I wrote. I wrote the stories of my Salvadoran friends that I had been sharing on the speaking tour. I wrote about my father and my attempts to understand both his suffering and the suffering of the Salvadoran people.

I sent my writing to a few friends, including Joan and Michael King. Michael, old friend from college, now Herald Press book editor, called several weeks later encouraging me to consider writing a book.

I decided to accept the challenge and started this book two weeks after my father's death. I was encouraged as it became clear that writing was a therapeutic process for me. Then I returned to El Salvador where, during the next few months, I experienced the war as never before. Already emotionally depleted, I felt as if the violence and death was about to overwhelm me. Sensing I had to get out, I went back to the U.S.

Writing was initially a convenient excuse for taking the time to deal with my own emotional issues. I could justify the "luxury" of being away from El Salvador because I was doing something "useful," something for "others." At the intellectual level I said from the beginning that writing was good for me. But it took several weeks to begin dismantling my emotional defense systems so I could recognize the extent to which I needed inner healing. I had to let go of writing for others and write for myself. I had to admit that dealing with my feelings was no luxury but essential to my emotional and spiritual health.

I stayed at the Loretto Motherhouse in rural Kentucky during the five most intense months of processing and writing. I'm grateful to the sisters who warmly welcomed me into their community, which was steeped in prayer and maturity. I'm particularly grateful for Elaine, Susan Carol, and Danielle, who each accompanied me in her own way as I relived my ten years in Latin America.

I returned to El Salvador thinking I was basically finished writing. When I learned Herald Press wanted extensive revisions, I was frustrated. My therapeutic process had ended. I was busy. Life had moved on. But with Michael's encouragement, I began to revise. Once more I started with the attitude that I was writing for others. I was encouraged as I made the cuts. It wasn't as hard as I had expected. The process confirmed that I had dealt with my emotions and had the distance necessary to decide what was essential to my story.

A week after I thought I had finished the revisions, I discovered the common thread weaving its way through my life. The thread is *contradictions*. God is challenging me to live out life's contradictions instead of trying to resolve them.

I don't understand the contradiction of hope resulting from suffering but the hope-filled people of El Salvador testify to the truth that "suffering produces perseverance; perseverance, character; and character, hope" (Rom. 5:3). Experiences with grief and death have helped me recognize, if still not understand, the contradiction of life springing from death. John 12:24 uses nature to describe it. "Unless a kernel of wheat falls to the ground and dies, it remains only a single seed. But if it dies, it produces many seeds." My own struggle with powerlessness has brought me face to face with the contradiction of a "power . . . made perfect in weakness" (2 Cor 12:9).

Writing has been a spiritual experience. I didn't start with what I wanted to say and then write it. I wrote, then sifted the words until I discovered what God's Spirit was trying to teach me. I'm thankful for the many people who supported me through this process, particularly for Kori, who encouraged me from the beginning. I'm also grateful for the friends who helped make this manuscript readable.

—*Susan Classen*
San Salvador, El Salvador

VULTURES & BUTTER- FLIES

1

Entering the Darkness

November 20, 1990
  Today is war. The possibility of my own death has never felt so real.

I sat writing by candlelight in a rural village in El Salvador, anxious to record the details of the day's dramatic events.

After spending several days in San Salvador, I left on the 6:00 a.m. bus for a meeting in the town of Chalatenango, close to my home. The bus ride was uneventful—until, about ten miles from our destination, we were stopped by an army truck blocking the road.

Soldiers told us to get off the bus and checked our documents. An officer asked if there were any foreigners. I stepped forward, concerned that he wasn't going to let me pass. I was relieved when he only asked if I was carrying a camera. Then the officer nonchalantly explained that there had been fighting in Chalatenango during the night but everything was under control.

We got back on the bus. Suddenly there were shots in the hills. People around me scrambled for cover. The driver began turning the bus around. I had about a minute to decide whether to get off the bus or not. I was debating when a woman I recognized came to me and suggested we get off together. Being with someone else seemed best so we got off along with about ten others.

We went to a nearby house where a number of people had gathered. After about a half hour of occasional gunfire, fifteen of us headed toward town. We met people sitting on the sidewalk in front of their houses a block below the barracks and convent where the fighting was taking place. Every once in a while shots came so close I could hear them whistling overhead.

I would not be able to go to the convent as planned. When two of the people I was with said they were going to the village of Guarjila, I decided to join them. Going to Guarjila was the next best thing to going home to Las Vueltas. As we headed toward the road to Guarjila, I was relieved, thinking we were leaving the fighting behind.

At the place where there is usually an army checkpoint, we began meeting wounded soldiers straggling into town. Some were walking; others were on horseback or carried in hammocks. The soldiers seemed scared and shaken.

We learned from people on the road that there had been fighting in Tepeyac, about a forty-five-minute walk away. As we walked, the couple from Guarjila and I discussed what to do. When we heard shots we waited until it was quiet, then went on.

Five minutes later there were shots so close I saw the gravel fly where the bullets hit. We ran back to a nearby house. There we waited until we saw a Red Cross ambulance arrive to evacuate five injured soldiers. I had counted twenty wounded soldiers since leaving town.

We had set off again and were on our way past the church when soldiers called us back. They took us to the porch of a house where an officer asked where we were going and checked our documents. He was quite pleasant given the circumstances but radioed our names in to the barracks.

He had just finished the call when the guerrillas attacked from a position directly in front of the open porch. The officer hit the dirt and began firing his weapon. He periodically shouted into his radio giving orders to the soldiers scattered around us. We crouched down with the officer behind the only protection available, a mud oven. The shooting probably didn't last more than fifteen minutes but seemed an eternity.

That night I wrote my thoughts in my journal.

> Caught in a military command post under attack! My main thought was "What a way to die!" It seemed such a foolish way to go. My heart was racing but my mind was functional. I mentally reviewed how I managed to get in that situation but couldn't think of any particularly unwise decision, given what we knew at the time.
>
> There was a wire basket hanging on a post beside me. I was absurdly aware that another round of shots had been fired—not just from hearing the deafening ringing in my head, but also from watching the basket jump and dance as the trembling ground shook the house. I felt the tension in my body as I helplessly waited for the impact of a bullet. Where would it hit? The thought of dying wasn't all that frightening but it surely seemed a waste to die in a military command post.

My feelings were numb as I thought back on the day's events. I wasn't yet in a safe environment that would allow the feelings to surface. Both my mind and body were on alert.

> I'll never forget the officer crouched in the dirt beside me. His cap was jauntily cocked on his head and sweat poured down his face. At one point our eyes met; he smiled. The wild look in his eyes faded for a moment. "¡Qué vida!" [What a life!] he said, shaking his head.

A Salvadoran military man and a North American pacifist, an unlikely pair. But we made a human connection as we both recognized the absurdity of war.

When the skirmish ended, another officer came over and they discussed what to do with us. They were tense and frightened and didn't want to be responsible for civilians, especially a foreigner. They urged us to return to Chalatenango.

We thanked them and hurried away, but at the road we made a quick decision to go on to the Guarjila. We were at the line of fire. Crossing it promised safety, whereas going back to Chalatenango would have meant returning through fighting.

We practically ran to a nearby store, passing a dead soldier on the way. At the store we received a warm welcome. After twenty minutes without shooting we went on. Our only concern was an A-37 plane that was dive bombing. Leaving the store we encountered another dead soldier and two hundred yards away a guerrilla patrol.

Just before Guarjila we passed a dozen vultures. I noticed them from far off and was afraid we would find another cadaver in the road. I never did see what they were after. As we got closer the vultures reluctantly flew to a nearby fence and I realized hundreds of yellow and white butterflies danced in that same area. We passed through their graceful flight.

> Vultures and butterflies. I was struck by the contrasting symbols of life and death. The vultures seemed so big and overpowering but the butterflies were there all along. I wondered about good and evil in my life. Do I let the evil loom so large that I miss the hundreds of small gifts of goodness?

In Guarjila I learned that the fighting wasn't just in this area. It was the start of a Salvadoran rebel military campaign, with simultaneous attacks all over the country. I continued to a neighboring village for the night and walked home to Las Vueltas the next day.

For the next several weeks I experienced war as never before. We did our best to care for the victims. Several stand out in my mind. There was Berta, age fourteen, who was killed by a mortar while working in her family cornfield. There was Ramón, a guerrilla combatant. And Martín, a government soldier. They were human beings in need of medical care. I was immersed in pain, suffering, and death without the protection of an emotional defense system to dehumanize people and turn them into the anonymous "enemy."

Ramón was one of our first seriously injured patients. Because of his condition our small rural clinic was used as an intensive care unit. The local health workers and I felt overwhelmed. I was a nurse. They were peasants with a first- or second-grade education, trained in basic disease prevention and treatment. We weren't prepared for patients like Ramón. At least Blanca, a doctor who worked in the area, was with us.

Ramón's jaw had been blown away by a bullet and Blanca decided she needed to operate. We prepared as best we could. We sterilized the instruments in a big can over an open fire, elevated a table on blocks of wood to serve as the operating table, and strung up an IV bottle with a rope tied to a ceiling beam.

It was midnight by the time the operation started. The shadows from the Coleman lantern danced eerily across the walls. One person held a flashlight so Blanca could see while others helped by handing her the instruments she requested.

The next morning Ramón was still recuperating from the anesthesia when he started hemorrhaging and stopped breathing. He needed an endotracheal tube to breathe through—but the only one we had was too big and Blanca couldn't get it down his throat.

The seconds ticked. In desperation Blanca finally did a tracheotomy. Since we didn't even have electricity, much less a respirator, I breathed for Ramón until he started breathing on his own again. This took about twenty minutes. The only thought on my mind was to breathe rhythmically into the tube, watch his chest rise, and get out of the way as his lungs compressed.

Blanca told me later that she had been so exhausted as we worked on Ramón that she felt as if she was above looking down on what was happening. As she watched me breathing into his tube, she said an image of my father flashed through her mind.

Dad had died three months earlier from a brain tumor and my emotions were still raw. I knew from my mother's death in 1981 that the grieving process is long and I wanted to give myself the time and space I needed to deal with Dad's death.

Once I returned to El Salvador after his funeral, though, I was swept away by the demands of my work. There was rarely an appropriate time to let my defenses down. I had become so accustomed to suppressing my emotions that I couldn't let the tears flow even when I had the opportunity.

Blanca's image of my father touched me deeply. Although it had been difficult, Dad had supported my being in El Salvador even during his eight-month illness. Breathing life into Ramón became a symbol reminding me that Dad's sacrifice had not been wasted.

The next afternoon two members of our team in San Salvador unexpectedly arrived in Las Vueltas. I knew co-workers would be concerned about me when they heard of the fighting in Chalatenango so I had asked a friend to call San Salvador as soon as she had access to a phone. I was shocked, however, when I learned what had taken place during the forty-eight hours before the call confirmed I was safe.

Just after the officer in Tepeyac had radioed the barracks with my name, the fighting started. An American military adviser was in the barracks when the call came. He saw my name and phoned the U.S. embassy with word that I had been detained and was under fire.

After hearing from the U.S. adviser, the embassy consul called our team directors. They spent the next two days looking for me. Friends began to wonder what the army was trying to hide after officials presented their fifth or sixth different version of what had happened. The situation had polarized. Either I was safely in Las Vueltas or I was in serious trouble, maybe dead. The emergency networks were notified and telegrams were sent on my behalf.

During the next few days I began to realize the stress was taking a toll. The threads were tangled: my personal grief, the tension of the military activity, overwhelming work demands at the clinic. I could only identify a sense of heaviness.

On what would have been my father's sixty-sixth birthday, I accompanied Gloria to the cemetery. Her son had just been killed and she wanted to visit his grave.

December 9, 1990
Gloria was so sad that just looking at her made me want to cry. But she mentioned several times that it was a comfort to know that her son's body had been properly buried and not left for the vultures.

When we got to the site Gloria said she didn't want a wooden cross because wood rots. Then a friend remembered that the men had stacked a bunch of old cement crosses in a pile when they cut the grass. Looking through the overgrown weeds, he found the crosses and chose one that was still in one piece and without a name. Another person volunteered to paint her son's name on it.

Gloria was pleased with a used gravestone. The poor don't even take burial and gravestones for granted!

Several days later, teenage Berta was killed. She and her brother were working in their cornfield when a mortar shot from the army base in Chalatenango exploded close by. That same day I rode back from San Salvador with the tiny casket of a two-year-old who had died of leukemia. On our way to the cemetery to bury Berta, we passed the corpse of a dead guerrilla. I felt as if death was battering me from all sides. I counted eleven deaths that had touched me personally during three weeks.

Experiencing both the FMLN rebel soldiers and the government soldiers as human beings made the reality of war and violence more difficult to deal with. Since the village where I lived was under FMLN control, I'd had more contact with the human side of the rebel combatants. Martín was a government soldier who reminded me that they, too, are human beings.

We took care of Martín in the clinic. I saw that he had a tattoo that said "Gladys." I asked if she was his girlfriend.

He was silent for a minute. Then said that she had been his girlfriend. But she had committed suicide when he was conscripted into the army ten months before.

What could I say? Martín was one of thousands of young men forced into the army. He has been on his way home when soldiers stopped the bus he was on and conscripted all able-bodied young men.

My emotional reserves were exhausted. I was losing my ability to cope. I was being enveloped in darkness. The military activity ended before Christmas and I had a little time to sort through what was happening to me.

> *December 20, 1990*
> I think I've identified part of what I need to deal with. The past month I've glimpsed a dark reality that influences everything around me. Evil, violence, pain, suffering, death. It's as though an abyss suddenly opened and darkness stared me in the face. But the abyss closed just as suddenly.

Now what do I do with it? Pretend it doesn't exist after all? If I allow myself to believe it does exist, then nothing on the surface can remain as it has appeared.

But this is Advent. A light shines in the darkness. A light slowly descends from on high illuminating the terrible shadows. Never have I felt the need for light or the power of the image as I do now. "O come, O come Emmanuel" is the heartfelt cry of my soul.

The darkness scared me. How close was I to being overwhelmed by it? What did I need in order to deal with it?

Mary Jo Leddy writes, "The darkness that dwells in our own subconscious can be unleashed by prolonged involvement in the sufferings of others."[1] To understand the darkness that had been unleashed, I had to go back to when I first began to experience suffering.

I started with my decision to go to Bolivia in 1981, my mother's illness and death, and the deaths of several of my Bolivian neighbors. Reading my journals, letters, and reports, I relived past experiences. I was taken aback by the intensity of feelings that emerged.

The closer I came to current experiences in El Salvador, the more time I needed to process my emotions. I needed a gentle environment to deal with my impotence, anger, and fear. I needed reflective space to feel the suffering of my Salvadoran friends and to grieve my father's death.

This story has emerged from my journey through such wounds. I risk sharing a story yet in process, a story so frustratingly real that it offers no solutions or definitive conclusions. I share it with the trust that, while the circumstances may be unique, the issues lie at the heart of human experience. And I share it with the hope that we will find wholeness as we humbly allow the threads of our lives to intertwine.

2

Called to Bolivia

It was July 25, 1981. The departure date had arrived and I was leaving for Bolivia. Five other new Mennonite Central Committee volunteers and I were in the Philadelphia airport on our way to Miami before continuing to Santa Cruz, Bolivia. Chris, Sue, and Trula, former housemates, had come to see me off as well as Joan with her newborn baby.

But the time for emotional good-byes had passed. Or had it? Maybe my feelings were just suppressed, buried down deep. Or was it God's grace enabling me to cope? I don't know. I know only I felt detached and distant.

Our flight was announced. Quick hugs all around. I boarded the plane. Seat assignments had been made and, by chance, the other volunteers were together and I was alone several seats behind. It was appropriate for how I felt. Alone. Isolated. Neither understanding myself nor feeling understood.

I sat back. A few tears escaped, belying my superficial sense of detachment. Two weeks earlier I had said good-bye to my mother who was dying of cancer. Would I see her again? If I did, under what circumstances? How long before I would be called home for her funeral?

At age twenty-three I was experiencing the reality of personal pain for the first time. My life had been unusually free of pain until the year before, when Mother was first diagnosed with breast cancer. I didn't know about the darkness of doubt, the anxiety of feeling out of control, or the tension of living with the unknown. I hadn't felt anger at injustice or fear of being pushed to the limit. I knew only I was embarking on a journey and was following God's call.

I grew up knowing that someday I would work overseas with the Mennonite Central Committee (MCC). My parents had worked with MCC in a children's home in France for ten years after World War II. Their values of service and openness to world needs shaped my childhood. They knew about letting go and moving on. They understood the richness of Christian values and Mennonite heritage beyond legalism and cultural trappings. And they accepted the personal sacrifice of promoting those values by giving me their blessing to work with the poor, even when my mother and nine years later, my father, were dying of cancer.

I graduated from Eastern Mennonite College in 1979 with a nursing degree and began working in a large hospital in Richmond, Virginia. After a year I grew restless. Nursing in a specialized intensive care unit was interesting and challenging but I was bothered by the ethical dilemmas. I watched families struggle with the painful choices afforded by advanced technology. Should they turn the respirator off and watch their loved one die or should they leave it on?

I was staggered by the cost of highly specialized medicine. We were spending hundreds of dollars a day to maintain patients declared brain dead while in other parts of the world children were dying from lack of basic antibiotics. I knew that cutting back on medical expenditures in the U.S. wouldn't help the children in the third world, but the decision of where to work was mine. I could choose to practice nursing someplace where even basic health care was unavailable.

The time seemed right to apply to MCC. I thought about where I might want to work. Bolivia had intrigued me since the evening I had listened to a former volunteer's tales of riding horses and motorcycles into remote villages to train health workers. I wasn't particularly interested in Africa or Asia and preferred learning Spanish to the Portuguese spoken in Brazil. I can't claim any highly spiritual motives for wanting to go to Bolivia. It sparked my sense of adventure!

My MCC application was being processed when my father called to say that Mother had found a lump in her breast; surgery was scheduled for the next day. It was June 1980. Under the influence of an environment where technology was god, I took for granted that, even if the lump was malignant, a mastectomy would solve the problem. Distance and the assumption that everything would be all right, because it had always been in the past, prevented me from dealing with reality even when my father called back to say Mother had cancer and the surgeons hadn't gotten it all.

I had been raised to be sensible but not paranoid or fearful about what life had to offer. My father's common sense had calmed many anxious people whose imaginations had run wild with all the bad things that could happen. But *his* practicality was tempered by the realization that bad things do sometimes happen. *I* was still naively assuming bad things wouldn't happen to me. My assumption was based on twenty-two years of experiencing life as positive and predictable. I hadn't yet learned that life is hard.

I moved back to Ohio in December to spend several months with family and to reconnect with my home church before leaving for Bolivia. As closely connected as I had been through letters and phone calls, I didn't deal with the reality of my mother's illness until I moved home. It seems to be a pattern that while I may be moved by hearing of someone's suffering, I'm not changed by it until directly involved.

Faith healing became an issue. I joined in the many fervent prayers for Mother's healing. When doubt raised its shadowy head, I quickly suppressed it. I feared that I would be to blame if she wasn't healed. But when I saw my mother struggling with the same issue, I began to resent the Christians who made a godly woman doubt her faith. How dared they imply it was her fault she wasn't healed? What kind of God did they pray to?

I was particularly struck by a woman with a false eye who insisted that God had healed her eye, even though years later she was still waiting to see the results. I didn't want anything to do with a theology that couldn't face the facts. So began an ongoing process of trying to understand what life teaches me about God.

Test results in March indicated that the cancer was spreading despite chemotherapy. Mother began a series of radiation treatments which caused side effects that made her progressively sicker. But she rarely complained. Her therapy was to go to the basement, turn on a tape recording of Scripture passages, and work on a quilt she was stitching for me. She had given my two older sisters quilts as wedding presents and was determined I would receive mine, too.

I felt guilty for still wanting to go to Bolivia. What were my motives? Was I trying to escape? I felt pressure from others. After all, I was a nurse, the youngest in the family, not married. It made sense for me to stay home. Yet my parents assured me of their support no matter what I decided.

On March 11 our church held a day of prayer and fasting for my mother. I spent the day praying about what I should do. After asking God to purify my heart, I wrote down my thoughts. What emerged was a sense of gratefulness that our family was surrounded by so much love and support. We were reaping the fruit of the love my parents had sown among many people in our young, suburban church. Those people were now anxious to repay the support Mother had offered so freely.

It struck me, however, that the best repayment I could make would not go directly to Mother but to those she had always tried to help, those who had no one else to support them. I felt God calling me to continue with my plans to go to Bolivia.

At the end of the day about fifty of us gathered and I shared my thoughts. The decision to go was sealed by tears of affirmation. It remains an example to me of the enabling function of the body of Christ. I was able to leave because others pledged to take my place at home.

But the testimony belongs primarily to my parents. "We dedicated you to God when you were a baby and we meant it," Dad said, his voice choked with emotion.

I knew that their highest value was for me to be faithful to God. They were able to let go of me and allow others to fill the gap.

The relief of making the decision was quickly replaced by the pain of carrying it out. With every new ache we wondered if the cancer was spreading. For the next five months we lived from one doctor's visit to the next. Sometimes there was good news, other times it was bad. But usually there was nothing to do but wait.

Waiting. Waiting. Always waiting. I felt as if I could handle bad news better than no news at all. If only I knew what I was dealing with! But then I would get down on myself. "What a jerk! Don't I love my mother? How can I prefer wanting to know something, anything over the limbo of waiting?"

It was hard to live one day at a time. It was hard not to fear the future. It was hard being home. It was hard being gone. It was hard to wait for news. It was hard to hear bad news. Those months were hard and there was no escape. I was learning life isn't always easy.

Once I arrived in Bolivia, I was caught up in the sights and sounds of a new and foreign place. Home and family slipped into the background, resurfacing with painful jolts whenever I received a letter or allowed my mind to wander.

The Bolivia MCC unit was large, with over forty volunteers plus children. The MCC center reminded me of a camp building with its bunk beds, hard mattresses, tile floors, and simple furnishings. I soon got used to the musty smell. The yard was a collage of jeeps, flowers, motorcycles, grass, horse wagons, and criss-crossing paths.

My second day in the country, I moved in with a Bolivian family with whom I was to live during the three months of language study. Although my "language school mother" was kind to me, I immediately noticed she couldn't talk to Sonia, the maid, without yelling.

Even middle-class families had maids since labor was cheap, I had been told. Cheap it was. When I had a chance to talk to Sonia alone I learned she earned the equivalent of $32.00 a month working six and a half days a week. Her belongings were kept in a small alley beside the house. She slept in the living room.

I was even more bothered that ten-year-old Reina seemed to be treated as a slave.

"Oh, she's an orphan girl we adopted," my language school mother explained when I asked about her. "We give her a place to live and send her to school in exchange for a little help around the house."

She obviously thought she was doing Reina a favor. But watching the little girl struggle with an impossible work load made me wonder.

Several days later I was in an adjacent room listening to my language school mother's normal tirade against Reina. Suddenly I realized she was beating her Reina with a wet leather belt. I cringed at every sharp crack against bare skin.

Shall I intervene? I asked myself. *If I get her to stop now will she just beat her harder once I'm gone? How can I reason with her when I can't even speak Spanish?* I was still trying to decide what approach to take when the beating stopped. Later I learned Reina was beaten because she was behind in her schoolwork, so I offered to help her. While I was learning that life was hard for me, I was also coming to understand that life was both hard and unfair for many others. How could I respond appropriately?

After an intense month of language study, we were to make our first trip to the outlying rural area known as the *campo*. I had picked up an interesting smattering of information about life in the mysterious world of the campo and was anxious to see for myself.

I knew that Nancy's legs, pocked with small, oozing sores from infected bites, were known as "campo legs" and that I could expect to look the same. I knew that Ron wore a flea collar around his ankle because there were lots of fleas in the campo. And that Andy scratched wherever and whenever he itched because that's what his neighbors did in the campo.

I learned that when MCCers arrived in their faded, mud splattered clothes they were just getting in from the campo. They would be full of stories about their trip to town which would invariably include something about fording a river, the jeep breaking down, or walking through mud. I also knew that our Spanish teachers were appalled to hear their former students nonchalantly speaking the vulgar vernacular they learned in the campo.

I went with Dean, Tim, and Deb to one of the recently opened MCC regions. The village of Nazaret had been settled five years earlier. About twenty-five families had moved from the densely populated mountains of the *altiplano* (high plains area) down to the tropical lowlands of Santa Cruz in search of land. They had requested a nurse and an agricultural worker. I was interested in the position because of the way MCC was working in that region. Faith and Liz lived in El Mocho, a half a mile away; Andy and Marlene lived two miles down the road in Galilea. We would work together as a team.

We made the sixty-mile trip in good time—about six hours of bouncing over the dusty, rutted roads. The visit passed quickly as I soaked up all I could. Used to camping, I had no trouble seeing myself living without electricity, running water, or indoor plumbing. I enjoyed the quiet evenings and the discussions about "our" work which made me feel like a real MCCer. Yes, this was a place I could belong.

Although we were expected back in Santa Cruz on Monday, we decided to wait until Tuesday so Andy wouldn't have to make a special trip to take us to the bus. Tim and Andy hopped on the motorcycle and went to Santa Rosa to call. We didn't want anyone to worry when we didn't show up on Monday.

When we heard the motorcycle returning to El Mocho, we hurried out to meet it.

"There has been another change of plans," Andy said, straddling the bike. He climbed off. "Susan, a telegram arrived for you on Friday."

My chest tightened.

"Your mother is worse but you don't necessarily need to go home yet."

I was stunned. I didn't expect it so soon. I knew from her two letters that she wasn't doing well but how could it happen so quickly?

It didn't take long to arrange to leave the next morning. I hardly slept that night. But when we left the next morning for the three-hour buggy ride to Santa Rosa, I was back to being fascinated with my surroundings. The gap between what was happening at home and what was happening around me was too big to bridge. I had to focus on one or the other.

We arrived in Santa Rosa around noon. I received my first introduction to crowded buses. It was the day after a big town fiesta so the visitors were on their way home. All the seats had been taken long before we arrived; even the aisles were jammed. We squashed and shoved our way through the hot, sweaty bodies and made a place for ourselves in the aisle. But it was so crowded that one time I picked my foot up and then couldn't find a spot to put it back down! We stood that way for an hour just waiting for the bus to leave.

Then it took two hours to travel the twenty-three miles to the paved road and another half hour to the next town where enough people got off to allow us some breathing room. I was amazed that no one was upset at what seemed to me to be almost intolerable conditions. The babies even slept!

We finally arrived in Santa Cruz in the early evening. As I walked into the MCC center my mind shifted back to home. By the time I was handed the telegram my hands were trembling. I felt as if I were a ball being bounced between two worlds. I opened the telegram and skimmed it quickly. It was worse than I expected.

I read it more carefully. "The cancer has spread to the liver . . . hospitalized . . . unable to walk or feed herself . . . mind frequently confused."

Sarah, a volunteer whose father had died of cancer several years earlier, went with me to call home through a ham radio operator. We got the call through but Dad wasn't home so we tried again later. This time we got through to my brother-in-law who told us where to call my father.

Eventually Dad's voice came over the radio, fuzzy but understandable. "The doctor said it could be days or weeks but she would not leave the hospital alive." I knew it was time to go home.

My mind was functioning but my feelings were numb. Knowing the inevitable will happen doesn't prevent the shock when it finally occurs. We began making arrangements for me to return to the U.S. but my passport was in La

Paz because of visa requirements. I didn't know how long I would have to wait.

My passport arrived the second day and I left that same evening. During the trip I thought about timing. I had only been in Bolivia five weeks. If I would have known that Mother was going to get worse so quickly I wouldn't have left when I did. But those five weeks were crucial in confirming that I wanted to work in Bolivia and that there were caring people to support me. Would I have gone if I had waited? I don't know.

I arrived home on September 3. Dad met me and we went straight to the hospital. I thought for a while that Mother was going to die that evening. It was hard watching her gasping and struggling for breath. Family and friends took turns staying with her around the clock and the cancer unit staff was understanding and flexible. Friday she seemed more relaxed as we stood around her bed singing the hymns she loved so much. Saturday morning she was alert. When the nurse asked if she knew I was home she responded, "Susie's here." Those were her last understandable words, a memory I cherish.

Saturday noon she took a turn for the worse. She died at 8:15 p.m. Dad and I were alone with her. Her death was not tranquil. I described it in my journal.

> After the last breath she let loose several grotesque moans. Her face was distorted, anything but peaceful and beautiful. The thoughts hurling through my mind were wild and confused. It was the worst death I've seen and I've witnessed a number.
>
> Where was God? What happened to the peace I've always heard about? It was awful. I was more torn and confused in those moments than I've ever been. But then she moaned once more and when I looked at her there was peace on her face.

I still wonder sometimes about those final moments. Initially, I tried to understand it from a spiritual perspective. Working nights in a nursing home, I had seen many people die. Many who were not necessarily Christians slipped peacefully away. My mother, who lived an exemplary Christian life, literally passed through the valley of the shadow of death. What did that mean?

I had no answer. I clung to the assurance that God is a God of life and to fight for life is a God-given instinct. She loved life and didn't give it up easily. She ultimately accepted death, but she never resigned herself to die.

Later I thought about her physical condition. The cancer had spread to her liver and liver failure can cause hallucinations and distorted images. What did she see and experience during those final moments? I was reminded that God doesn't fit in a box. We can't draw definitive spiritual conclusions from isolated events. Christians don't necessarily die one way and non-Christians another.

The following days passed in a haze of tears, hugs, cards, and visitors. Once the funeral was over, Dad and I took my sister back to her home in Kansas. We appreciated the opportunity to be together in the car and I enjoyed hearing him reminisce. I don't think we talked about it, but I sensed that we needed each other in a special way. My sisters had their husbands and families. My father and I had only each other. Leaving him alone in the airport when I returned to Bolivia was one of the hardest good-byes I have ever said.

3

Death and Mysterious Grace

My eyes roamed the room. "Can this be called a clinic?" I wondered. It was small, about eight by ten feet. The uneven dirt floor looked like a topical map full of bumps and dips. Chunks of dried mud had fallen here and there from the walls, revealing bamboo slats that had been plastered over with a mud-grass mixture. A weathered table sat in one corner of the dark, windowless room. A slightly lopsided set of shelves holding a few basic medicines stood propped against the wall. There wasn't even a bed.

Pablo, age twenty-six, a patient who had arrived the night before, was lying on a straw mat. I watched the rapid rise and fall of his chest. Respirations, sixty per minute. Twenty is normal. He didn't have much fever but his pulse was rapid. Family members said he had been vomiting for five days; his muscular body was shrunken from dehydration.

Coming from a small, jungle village, his relatives had been relieved when they arrived at the little clinic in Galilea. The primitive surroundings didn't look like much to me but I was comparing it to the intensive care unit where I used to work. They were comparing it to what was available in their village—nothing.

Suddenly Pablo's respirations changed, bringing my mind back to the present. He gasped. Heart pounding, I knelt beside him. I desperately wished Ethel and Marlene, the two experienced nurses, would hurry back. I propped him on my knee, hoping he would breathe easier. *I'm only visiting Marlene*, I kept thinking. *I haven't even started my assignment yet.* The situation seemed unreal.

One more breath and his body went limp. My hands were trembling. I could hardly still them enough to feel for his pulse. But it didn't matter. He was dead. My mind reeled as I slowly laid him down on the mat.

What a contrast with my mother, who had died six weeks earlier surrounded by the best of medical technology. Here, a strong, healthy young man died because no medical care was available. It was unfair. It shouldn't have happened. It didn't need to have happened. Was there something else we could have done? I was still stunned when Ethel and Marlene arrived a few minutes later.

My family's experience with illness and death contrasted sharply with the experiences of my Bolivian neighbors. Gregoria's death some time later was significant as I reflected on the relationship between poverty and health.

I was at home in Nazaret when a woman came to say that my next door neighbor, Gregoria, was sick and couldn't stop vomiting. I went to the house, where I was told that Gregoria had swallowed Gramaxone. I knew only that Gramaxone is a slow-acting herbicide. I didn't know what might happen to Gregoria once it absorbed into her system.

We hitched up the horses and started on the three-hour trip to the hospital. Celestino, Gregoria's husband, went along as well as two other community men. As we traveled, I asked what had happened. Celestino seemed angry and wouldn't say anything.

"She tried to kill herself because she and Celestino had a fight," quietly explained one of the men making sure

Celestino couldn't hear. "She was angry because he hit her."

"Why did he hit her?" I asked.

"She was the only woman who kept going to the oil drilling camp after we told them to stop," he replied.

As we plodded along I had time to think about what I had
been told. The oil drilling camp had moved into our area
several months earlier. The huge machines, trucks, and men
a half mile away caused quite a commotion in our quiet village. Excitement ran high as we speculated about the discov-
ery of an oil reserve practically in our back yard.

But the women of the village discovered a more immediate reward. They found that leftover food from the camp
kitchen was dumped in a ditch by the road. Each day
brought hope of a new delicacy: bread from the city, some
cake still wrapped in plastic, a piece of meat. The women
knew nothing about economics, the 500 percent inflation
rate, or why peasant farmers couldn't get ahead no matter
how hard they worked. They knew only that they had nothing to feed their families besides rice. What was garbage to
the men in the camp was a feast for the village children.

Their husbands weren't so enthusiastic. It insulted their
pride to think of "their" women digging through garbage for
food scraps. It touched a sore spot, painfully reminding
them of their inability to put enough food on the table. A
community meeting was called. All the men gathered and
quickly reached a decision. They would forbid their wives to
go to the camp.

A week later another meeting was called. "Celestino, your
wife is the only one still going to the camp. It makes the
whole village look bad." The pressure on Celestino was intense. His image as a man was at stake. All the men in the village were evaluating who was boss—he or his wife. After the
meeting, Celestino went home determined to lay down the
law. They fought. Gregoria refused to obey. He hit her.
Fighting back the only way she knew how, Gregoria drank

the herbicide. Her husband would not have the last word.

It was almost midnight by the time we reached the small hospital staffed by an unsupervised, first-year intern. The doctor examined her and admitted her for observation. He wasn't worried. She could probably be discharged by Tuesday. Celestino stayed with Gregoria and the rest of us went back to Nazaret.

I was relieved that the doctor thought she would be all right. But by this time I had enough experience to know I couldn't trust the care she would receive at the hospital. Tuesday evening Celestino arrived after carrying Gregoria the last two miles on his back. I went to see her. She looked terrible.

"She seemed worse to me so I insisted that the doctor examine her before he left for Santa Cruz," Celestino explained. "He said she was ready to be discharged. What else could I do?"

By Wednesday morning she was worse. Her face and neck were swollen. Her lips were raw. She was disoriented and agitated. The health promoter said she had been vomiting all night. "Her vomit looks like raw hamburger," the promoter graphically offered. Her condition was critical. Was there hope if we took her back to the hospital? Probably not, but we couldn't watch her die without trying something.

The whole community was involved by this time. One of the horses had gone lame so we couldn't take her in the wagon. The men tied a hammock to a bamboo pole and set out walking.

Gregoria died as they arrived at the hospital. I was angry with the doctor for discharging her in the first place. He was on his way to the city. Is that why he sent her home? I tried to give him the benefit of the doubt. Maybe he knew she would have died anyway and wanted to let her die at home. But he could have at least explained to Celestino. Or maybe he didn't know any more about Gramaxone poisoning than

I did and honestly thought she was okay. After all, the medical training the doctors receive is sporadic and inadequate.

Why did Gregoria die? Why was she so poor that she had to dig through garbage in search of food? Why did the men make decisions for their wives to obey unquestioningly? Why didn't she receive adequate treatment in the hospital?

Grieving my mother's death made me more sensitive to others and prepared the ground for questioning why people like Gregoria died. But I didn't know much about the grieving process and was unaware of how it was affecting me. I dealt with it as something I should get over.

I would get frustrated with myself. Why was I teary on my birthday two months after Mother's death and vaguely depressed at Christmas? I didn't identify my unpredictable emotions as a normal part of the grieving process. I simply pushed myself and did the best I could.

My experiences with poverty and death in Bolivia defied simple explanations. I began to think about relationships among God's children. Perhaps some don't have enough because others have more than they need. Compared to my Bolivian friends I was clearly among those with more than enough. I felt humbled. A personal health crisis in August 1983 brought the issue into sharper focus.

Chon and Juliana brought their eighteen-month-old son, Demetrio, to the clinic with a cough and fever. I gave him some medicine and he improved. But the next morning he started convulsing. My efforts to bring down his soaring temperature were futile and the convulsions continued.

"He has to go to the hospital," I explained to his parents.

There was even a ride available saving them the four or five hour walk. But they hesitated.

"There is nothing more I can do for him here," I insisted, not understanding their reluctance.

Chon looked down as he scuffled his feet in the dust. "Our oldest daughter is also sick," he said uncomfortably.

"She has fever and diarrhea. What with inflation and all, we didn't get much for the rice we harvested."

There was a moment of silence. He looked up at his wife, Juliana, as I wondered what all this had to do with Demetrio.

Chon continued. "We have to think of our five other children," he said with a glint of defensiveness in his voice.

Suddenly I understood. My heart ached at their dilemma. There wasn't enough money. Should they spend the little they had on the oldest who wasn't very sick but had a good chance for recovery? Or should they spend it on the youngest whom they thought would probably die anyway?

Could they live with themselves if they watched Demetrio die without doing anything? If they spent their money trying to help him and then had to watch their other children go hungry until the next rice harvest? The truck left as they agonized over the decision.

The next morning a pickup pulled into the village. I hurried to Chon and Juliana's house to tell them there was another chance to go to the hospital. They decided to take the oldest daughter. But five minutes later Juliana came rushing after the truck with Demetrio in her arms. Her life-giving maternal instinct couldn't live with the decision to do nothing. I breathed a sigh of relief but my heavy heart told me it was probably too late.

I heard the sound of a motor several hours later and poked my head out the door. The infrequent passing of a vehicle was always worth watching. It was the same truck. Juliana climbed out carrying the lifeless form of her son.

I had seen so many people die during my two years in Bolivia that I was familiar with the funeral rituals. Neighbors gathered immediately to help. The women washed Demetrio's body, wrapped him in clean white rags, and laid him on a table placed in the middle of their small mud house. The men searched here and there until they found the scraps of wood they needed to make the tiny coffin. The children gathered flowers which they placed carefully around his corpse, leaving only his face visible. They folded his stiffened hands together and stuck a flower between them. Four candles were lit, one on each corner of the table.

Feeling useless, I went home to rest before the all-night vigil. I never stayed all night at the wakes. Only the men did that, drinking and playing cards. I went back in the evening and sat on one of the crude, wooden benches borrowed from the neighbors.

A few people talked quietly. Children ran in and out, occasionally stopping to stare at the body. No one looked very upset. Bolivians are used to children dying. I couldn't understand at first why they waited months before naming their babies. Then a friend explained that they wait until reasonably sure the baby will live before bothering with a name.

Juliana entered carrying a gourd bowl with an alcoholic beverage which was passed from person to person, each one taking a sip. I touched it to my lips so I wouldn't offend them but didn't actually swallow the fiery drink. I didn't like it under the best of circumstances and with my stomach feeling queasy all afternoon, the thought of drinking it made me nauseated. By 9:30 I was feeling worse so I excused myself and went home.

Sure enough, diarrhea hit that night. Intestinal problems are so common I thought of it as only a bother. I had to get up four or five times and by morning barely made it out the door of my house before I vomited.

Straightening up, I gasped as an excruciating pain tore through my right, lower side. I blinked back the tears that involuntarily filled my eyes and took several deep breaths. Yes, I could make it back to bed if I took it slow. On my way past the bookshelf I grabbed my favorite health care guide, *Where There Is No Doctor*. I looked up appendicitis. All the symptoms fit. Now what?

I took stock of my situation. Tim, the MCC agronomist

who lived within shouting distance, was in Santa Cruz. The other village houses were across the soccer field. Would anyone hear if I shouted? I sighed with relief when I remembered Faith was coming after the horse that morning.

It seemed an eternity before I heard Faith's friendly "Good morning" outside my window.

"Come in here a minute," I replied as calmly as I could.

She walked into the house and immediately noticed my strained expression. "What's wrong? Do you have cramps again?" she asked, since I often had trouble with painful menstrual cramps.

"Not this time," I said. "I think I have appendicitis."

Her face turned so white I forgot myself and began to laugh. But the pain instantly reminded me of my predicament and the chuckle died as quickly as it came. Knowing that I would have to wait several hours while Faith made contact on the MCC radio, I had her give me two *novalginas,* a strong pain killer that Bolivians use for everything. Then she galloped off so fast that I was sure she would fall and break her neck! I prayed that she would make it to Galilea where Brian and Marcy lived.

The pain medication quickly took effect and I began to feel so good that I was sure I was okay after all. I was embarrassed that I was getting everyone excited for nothing.

Before long I heard the motorcycle; Brian pulled up with Faith on the back. The message had been communicated by radio and emergency plans were being made. Now I almost hoped I did have appendicitis, since I was causing so much commotion. The priest from nearby Santa Rosa had an airplane but he wasn't home. The volunteers in Santa Cruz thought they would be able to find another mission plane so it seemed best for me to go to the landing strip in Galilea.

Faith and Brian had already arranged for the store owner to take me to Galilea in his truck. I climbed gingerly into the cabin with Faith at my side, still wondering if I was in enough pain actually to have appendicitis. The three miles to Galilea took about twenty minutes. As we arrived at Brian and Marcy's house, we heard the drone of a plane. Marcy hurried out, scanning the sky. Yes, it was the priest from Santa Rosa. No, they hadn't communicated with him.

The plane came to a bumpy halt on the grassy strip. The priest, knowing nothing of our situation, had simply arrived for his monthly visit! It was a miracle. He willingly agreed to fly us to Santa Cruz. There was only one seat besides the pilot's, so Faith climbed in the back. I sat between her knees.

Once airborne, the little plane felt like a defenseless kite blown back and forth by every shift in air current. The miracle pain killer began wearing off; I felt sicker and sicker.

"Faith!" I yelled, trying to make myself heard over the roar of the engines. "Do you have a plastic bag?"

The priest, well prepared for such emergencies, heard me and handed one back. I heaved into the bag, trying not to miss as the plane swooped and dropped in the wind. Hyperventilating from the pain and nausea, I felt my hands beginning to cramp until I could hardly move my fingers. Then I heard Faith gagging behind me.

"The bag!" she said desperately.

I quickly handed her the half-full bag, barely able to force my cramped fingers to release it.

"The air is so hazy we're not going to be able to land in Santa Cruz," the priest shouted above the noise. "I'll take you to the hospital in Portachuelo instead."

My heart sank. *Portachuelo!* I thought to myself. *No way!* I had visited that hospital once—small, dirty, under-equipped, first-year interns the only doctors. All noble ideals of identifying with the poor were thrown aside. I wasn't going to the hospital in Portachuelo!

I suggested that if we landed there the MCCers could pick me up and take me the hour drive to Santa Cruz. Then the priest remembered a small landing strip closer to the city.

We finally drew close to the strip, circled, and landed. But no one was there to meet us. Now what? Fortunately, by the time I was out of the plane Tim and Larry had arrived.

I crawled in the back and lay down, no longer questioning if something was wrong. Every stop and start sent pain shooting through my body. It felt as if fluid was sloshing around in my abdomen. We were at the clinic by 10:00 a.m. I was finally in good hands. The doctor was trained in the U.S. and had his own clinic which was well-staffed and equipped. Although he laughed at my self-diagnosis, he soon confirmed it and surgery was scheduled for 12:00 noon.

The operation went well. But when the doctor came back the next morning with the lab reports he looked more serious than he had earlier. The appendix was already gangrenous and necrotic. Purulent fluid had drained into my abdomen, so he was giving me high doses of antibiotics to prevent an infection. He had never removed an appendix so close to rupturing. It usually takes two days to reach that point and I only had severe pain for six hours.

"You are a very lucky young woman!" he exclaimed.

I had time to reflect while I recuperated. The care I received contrasted sharply with the care available to Demetrio. Why did I live when Demetrio died? Why were the best medical facilities in the country at my disposal? I didn't think it was just coincidence that the priest flew into Galilea right when I needed him. I believed it was God's grace. But why me?

The mystery of God's grace is just as real as the mystery of suffering. I can't glibly proclaim God's miraculous protection and still look people like Demetrio's parents in the eye. I can only humbly confess that God gave me a gift of grace which I don't understand or deserve.

4

Powerless to Be Present

After two years in Bolivia I needed to decide whether I wanted to stay longer than my original MCC commitment. I was toying with the idea of extending.

One afternoon I was in the MCC center in Santa Cruz catching up with news on the bulletin board. I glanced at some announcements and browsed through a Christmas letter someone had posted. The letter caught my interest; I read it more carefully. An MCC nurse in Guatemala was describing her visit to El Salvador. She had been asked to help decide if MCC should start a health program in that war-torn country. Moved by her experience, she ended her Christmas letter with an appeal for someone willing to work in El Salvador.

I read the letter twice. Then I took it off the bulletin board, sat down, and read it again. I didn't understand why I was so affected. My practical mind overruled my heart, which seemed to be saying I was the one to go. It was out of character for me to follow spontaneous urges and God had never led me through that kind of mystical quickening of the Spirit.

I didn't say anything to anyone. How could I explain that I thought maybe I was supposed to go to El Salvador just because of a letter on the bulletin board? I knew nothing about El Salvador except what I had read in *Newsweek*. The only step I took was to make an appointment to talk to Herman Bontrager, our Latin American director, when he came to visit several months later. I said I wanted to talk to him about extending my term in Bolivia.

"Would you be open to other options in Latin America?" Herman asked in his slow, deliberate manner.

"Maybe," I said carefully wondering what options he would present. He went on to mention several openings.

"But there is one," he said, "that is particularly challenging. We need someone with experience who already speaks Spanish."

My heart began to pound. Was he going to suggest El Salvador?

"We are looking for two nurses to go to El Salvador," Herman paused. A shiver went up and down my spine. "It's always hard to know how to recruit for a position that may involve so much risk."

My hands were sweaty. I'm sure my voice was shaking as I explained that I had been thinking about El Salvador ever since I read a letter about it. We were both moved by a clear sense of God's Spirit.

The decision was processed during the next few months. I prepared to leave Bolivia two months early to begin work in El Salvador—and left in October of 1983. I experienced many emotions during those weeks. Sadness at leaving Bolivia, excitement about spending time with family and friends in the U.S., enthusiasm and apprehension about starting in El Salvador. I didn't even think about the issues I would face during my two-month home leave.

I arrived home the day before my father's wedding. His fiancée, Donna, was a family friend from way back. Dad had written about their relationship as it developed and I was excited for them. When he visited me in Bolivia I realized how lonely he was. Knowing he had someone to share his life with made it easier for me to make another commitment to MCC. So I went home excited about a happy family celebration.

Dad and Donna met me at the airport and we drove home talking enthusiastically. They filled me in on wedding plans and Dad's move to Donna's house several blocks from our home on Curtis Drive. We pulled into the driveway and I took everything in just as I had always done coming home from college. The picket fence had been taken down, the garage door needed painting, new bushes had been planted—all the small details of the house I had lived in all my life.

We went in. I was home! But I felt as if I had been hit with a blast of cold air. The house was practically empty. My home was an empty shell. I was stunned as Dad continued his animated explanation of how he had distributed the furniture and household items.

"Christine has the dining room table, Dave took the bedroom suite. Oh yes, and Miriam has the good china. . . ."

I just nodded my head as it sunk in for the first time in two years that Mother was dead. I went to bed with a heavy heart.

But it was impossible to stay that way with all the excitement. I soon suppressed the grief that had popped out so unexpectedly and joined the festive wedding spirit. When Dad and Donna were on their honeymoon, I borrowed a car and left to visit old friends from college.

After we were all back, though, the feelings engulfed me. No one had discussed where I was going to stay. Would I stay with Dad and Donna? Would I stay in our old home?

I was angry at my father. He knew I was going to be home. Didn't he even think about where I would stay? When we talked, though, I glimpsed the pain he had been dealing with since Mother's death, the pain that came through in letters only as hints. I was suddenly struck by how hard the past two years had been for him. And I realized that loss isn't something that one gets over with in a year or two.

I felt selfish when he explained that *he* was feeling displaced, too. Although happily remarried, he was adjusting to a new home that didn't feel as if it was his yet. He cried when he said he felt torn between his daughter and his new wife. He didn't know what to do, so he didn't do anything.

But being a thoughtful, sensitive person, Donna lost little time in inviting me herself. It all worked out and I learned a painful lesson about grief's unexpected twists and turns.

During the weeks that followed I tied up the loose ends at our old home, sorting through Mother's letters from France, pictures, papers, and so forth. Her most personal belongings had been boxed up when the house was cleaned out.

Grief manifested itself in a number of ways during that time. Sometimes I was angry. Why weren't my two sisters doing more to help? At times I felt privileged to receive personal glimpses into my mother's life. Then there was the guilt. Was I right to have left for Bolivia when I did? I remembered the times my own struggle with her illness kept me from supporting her as I wanted. I felt ashamed. Why hadn't I tried harder? I felt cheated that I didn't really get to know her as an adult. Now that I had some of my own MCC stories to tell I wished I could listen to hers.

Those two and a half months were difficult but positive. When January 1984 rolled around I was excited about opening a new chapter in my life.

Maureen, my new co-worker, and I went to MCC orientation and on to Guatemala for a month of language refresher. Our assignment was to develop a health program at the request of a community of five Poor Clare nuns and three Franciscan priests in the parish of San Francisco Gotera, Morazán. Two MCC volunteers had been there for several months in 1983 assessing the situation and trying preliminary ideas. They found enthusiastic participants for health work and recommended longer-term MCC involvement.

It was March by the time we arrived in Gotera ready to jump in and get to work. Bolivia had provided many opportunities for discussing development issues, so I thought I had realistic expectations for work in El Salvador. I was satisfied that even if I couldn't solve the problems, I would be there with the people as we shared and learned together. We talked about it in terms of "projects versus presence."

Because of the obstacles presented by the war, I went to Gotera with low expectations for successful projects. But I was confident that I could at least be present with people in their suffering. It came as a rude awakening to find that I couldn't even be present in the way I had anticipated.

Gotera is the capital of Morazán province, one of the areas hardest hit by the war. In 1980 and 1981, thousands of people fled their homes. Some went north, to become refugees in Honduras, while others went to Gotera, where they lived in three camps for the displaced. Gotera mushroomed from a sleepy town of about 6,000 to include an additional 12,000 displaced civilians and 3,000 soldiers.

The military presence pervaded the whole town and we lived in the heart of it. The new barracks took over the church garden. Its foreboding wall loomed like an ominous shadow over the convent where Maureen and I lived. Our street was blocked on two sides by yellow barricades announcing "STOP. Military Zone." A soldier on guard duty outside our house was a constant reminder of our location.

Even inside the house it was impossible to forget our surroundings. Often in the evenings, army trucks would park outside, loading up soldiers on their way to military operations. Some people said the soldiers were drugged. Others said it was psychological hype.

I only knew that they whooped and hollered as they

climbed on the trucks cocking their guns. Sometimes they grunted like animals. Their faces were painted for war. Most would simply smear on the green paint. But others heightened the savage effect by adding stripes of black or red or using different shades of camouflage colors.

There were several incidents of guns accidentally going off while the soldiers prepared to leave. Even though I knew intellectually that the guns were real, I didn't feel it in my gut until I began to experience their destructive power first hand. Once a bullet entered the priests' house, slamming into a closet where one priest had been standing just moments earlier. The only damage was a bullet hole through one of his shirts.

The doctor's secretary wasn't as lucky. She was hit in the arm as she sat at her desk. Then there was the time in the middle of the night when one of the guards in front of our house accidentally shot his buddy.

I soon realized I couldn't be present in the way I had found rewarding in Bolivia. There, I naturally related to my neighbors as we shared our lives through walking, drawing water at the well, visiting. Sometimes in Bolivia I longed for privacy as curious neighbors stood at the door of our mud house gawking. We thought we were living simply but their stares reminded us that we had numerous possessions they had never seen.

Now that I was living in the privacy of convent walls, I realized I felt cut off from the people with whom I wanted to relate. There was almost no neighborly interaction. It seemed no one came to visit unless they wanted something from us. But I wasn't in Bolivia. I was in El Salvador, where many factors beyond my control determined where and how I could be present.

One factor was the relationship between the army and the church. When I arrived the colonel was frustrated that the 200-year-old church building was inconveniently located in the middle of his military compound! He wanted the church torn down and rebuilt some other place.

The parish team was also concerned that if the convent were left empty the army would take it over as they had the other houses on the block. Our presence there may not have met my desire to share my life with the poor but it did make a statement to the military. I came to see it as symbolic of our struggle to define the church's role in the midst of political turmoil and violence.

The sounds of war are indelibly imprinted on my mind. Every morning at 4:30 or 5:00 a.m., the soldiers would do their exercises outside our door. I can still hear the stomping boots as the soldiers ran past in rhythm, and the jangle of the guns that never left their sides. They would chant as they ran. "We are soldiers strong and brave. We will kill the communists. We will drink their blood." Then they would stop and do push-ups and deep knee bends, the officer gruffly counting "Uno, dos, tres, cuatro. Uno, dos, tres, cuatro." At 6:00 a.m. and 6:00 p.m. the band played the national anthem, accompanied by the soldiers' off-key singing.

Periodically, usually at night, cannons would shoot mortars into the surrounding countryside. The house would shake with each discharge. I eventually stopped jumping when an unexpected explosion shattered the night. My only reaction was to clench my teeth, physically suppressing the sudden wrench in my gut that I managed to hide but not conquer.

I learned to wait 10 or 15 seconds listening for a distant explosion as the mortar landed 10 or 20 kilometers away. I also learned to ask the next day where it had landed and if anyone had been injured. The deadly projectiles hurling through the dark terrorized the families living in the countryside.

I absorbed bits and pieces of information, trying to understand what the war was about, how it started, why church workers were targeted. It didn't take much astute analysis, though, to realize that Maureen and I wouldn't be able to do good development work when it was too dangerous even to visit some of the neediest communities, much less work there.

I tried to resign myself to concentrating our work in Gotera. After all, there were over 12,000 displaced people there and plenty of health needs to keep us busy. But it was hard. Instinct told me we should be working with families in the countryside, helping them to stay in their homes. True, the displaced in Gotera had many needs but they also had more resources available.

When we arrived in Gotera, we took over the parish pharmacy. There was a public hospital in town, newly built with U.S. funds. But it was staffed by doctors straight from medical school, fulfilling their obligatory year of social service. They worked with little or no supervision. Few were motivated to serve the poor. The medicine supply was limited and soldiers received priority over civilians. As a result, patients flocked to the convent with their prescriptions. The church was their last hope since they had no money to buy the expensive medicines.

I struggled with the pharmacy program from the standpoint of community development. If the hospital were doing its job, we wouldn't have to be handing out medicines. Why didn't the hospital have medicines, anyhow? Was it corruption, disorganization, military dominance? Weren't we bailing out a faulty system, letting them off the hook, instead of dealing with the root of the problem?

We decided to look for someone else to work in the pharmacy so Maureen and I could concentrate on health education in the camps. Ana Mariá, an active church member, began working in June 1984. I was enthusiastic about having more time to spend in El Tiangue, a camp of about 2,000 people housed in shacks on the edge of town. Maybe I couldn't live there or solve their health problems but I could at least listen to them, give them a chance to express their thoughts and feelings. After all, that's what presence is about. I was to receive another rude awakening.

A young woman who came to us for help made me realize people were afraid even to talk about their past, much less express their thoughts and feelings. Maureen answered the knock at our door.

The woman standing there was obviously tense. "I'm . . . uh . . . displaced. I . . . I . . . don't have food for my children. Please, can you help me?" She twisted her hands nervously as Maureen invited her in.

"What happened that forced you to leave your home?"

Her eyes filled with tears. "Last week the soldiers killed my husband. No! No!" She stopped terrified. "I mean the guerrillas killed my husband."

To tell the truth was to invite her own death. Her survival among the same soldiers that killed her husband depended on her blaming the guerrillas. I felt bad that Maureen and I had even asked.

Not wanting to make people uncomfortable with my questions, I asked the nuns about the background of those living in El Campo, another camp for the displaced. I learned it was made up mostly of people who had fled the Mozote area.

"Mozote." My ears perked up at hearing the name. I had heard that in December of 1981 soldiers from the Atlactl battalion massacred the entire population of Mozote, over 900 men, women, and children. I could hardly believe it when Sister Anselma said that word of the massacre had only leaked out like a slow trickle. How could it be that of the thousands of people who fled the surrounding areas, no one came forth to denounce publicly the barbaric slaughter? The priests and nuns only came to realize that something terrible had happened because of the sudden influx of people into Gotera.

The majority were evangelicals, but from the relatively few Catholics who arrived, the parish priest soon had a list of over 225 names to be mentioned in prayers for the dead. They would arrive saying, "Padre, will you please say mass for my mother and my sister, and for my brother and his three children?" Finally a journalist went to investigate and the *New York Times* broke the story of the Mozote Massacre.

By this time I was frustrated. Innocent questions like, "Where are you from?" and "What brought you here?" were off limits. They brought up a past that people were trying to suppress. Who was I to say that it was destructive for them to bottle up their feelings? Could I guarantee the physical and emotional space necessary to deal with their trauma? Could I guarantee their safety if they told the truth about atrocities committed by the army?

By the time I arrived in Gotera most of the displaced had achieved their one main goal: survival. My need to be "present" in a meaningful way would only disturb the precarious equilibrium they had achieved. I felt impotent. I couldn't even be an active listener.

5

The Politics of Manipulation

Never having paid much attention to politics, I had a lot to learn when I got to El Salvador. Arriving at election time, I realized from the beginning that no one was immune from the effects of political maneuvering.

I had been working for several months in a camp of about 2,000 displaced people. Housing consisted of long tin-roofed structures partitioned off into family units. The tin had been supplied by the parish but each family was responsible for the rest. The walls consisted of a hodge-podge of plastic, cornstalks, rocks, or mud. Infectious diseases were rampant.

My co-worker Maureen and I had started classes two Saturdays a month with six health promoters, two from each of the three camps. The health promoters were given a few basic medicines such as aspirin, Tylenol, and cough syrup which they distributed to people who came to them. But we were quite aware that handing out medicines wasn't enough. We had to do something to control the spread of respiratory infections, intestinal parasites, measles—so we also started general preventive health classes for larger groups.

I enjoyed preparing the classes, experimenting with different teaching methods and creative ideas. The group of ten in El Tiangue was enthusiastic and we had fun together. I was starting to realize, though, that the education "trickle-down theory" wasn't working. They weren't supposed to be in the class just for themselves. They were supposed to be motivating their friends and neighbors to improve their health habits.

One problem we had identified from the beginning was that many people weren't using the latrines. I arrived for class one afternoon determined to develop a concrete plan of action. The week before we had discussed promoting an education campaign about health hazards of human waste. The assignment for this week was to think of ways to implement such education.

"Okay. What ideas have you thought of?" I asked once the group was settled.

"We could do skits after mass," Carlos said. I nodded my head and encouraged more brainstorming.

"How about something in the school?" another suggested.

"We could each meet with our neighbors and give a talk like they used to in the clinics," Lupe suggested.

I was interested in her comment about the clinics. "Did they give classes in the health clinic?" I asked.

"Sure," Lupe responded. "While we waited to see the doctor, the nurses would give talks about the importance of latrines, not going barefoot, boiling drinking water, and other things like that."

"Do you think most of the people here have heard those classes some time or another?" was my next question.

"Of course," several responded.

My premise was that people weren't using the latrines because they didn't understand their importance. This new piece of information was throwing doubt on my assumption that an education campaign would get people to change their habits. "So if people already know that they should use latrines, why don't they do it?"

They looked at each other, embarrassed by the subject matter.

Carlos was first to speak. "People who have lived in the campo all their lives aren't used to them," he said. "When it's just one family surrounded by cornfields, it's just easier . . . Well, you know. . . ."

Several women giggled.

"They just aren't used to using them even if they've been taught differently," he finished quickly.

"So how do we convince them to change?" I asked.

"I think we should drill it into their heads," Lupe said. "The education campaign is a good idea."

Lucia wasn't so sure. "Have you gone near the latrines in this camp?" she asked.

I had to admit I hadn't.

"They stink!" she exclaimed. "We all know people who aren't used to them sometimes make a mess. What's more, there's dirty paper and corncobs lying all over the place. I don't blame people one bit for not using those awful latrines."

We all agreed she had a good point. *Now we're on to something,* I thought to myself. I asked who was responsible to clean the latrines.

"Toño's supposed to," Carlos said. "He's even getting paid for it. But he only works when he feels like it."

Mariá spoke for the first time. "That's true, but you can hardly blame him when he doesn't get paid regularly."

The others nodded.

"Who's responsible for paying him?" I asked.

The president of the camp council was supposed to collect a fee from each family and give the money to Toño. But the president was lax in collecting the money because he was upset that the other council members weren't doing their share of the work. On top of that, people were accusing him of misusing the funds. Understanding why people weren't using the latrines was getting complicated.

"What can we do to get the council to function better?"

Silence.

I knew the parish team had been working hard with the camp councils. The camps in Gotera were some of the best organized in the country, at least until the government took over right before elections.

"If the council isn't functioning, why don't you change it?" I wondered.

"It was just changed," someone finally explained. "After the elections, the new governor appointed members of her political party to the council."

The subject changed. Our class ended with no solution to the latrine problem. I wasn't politically astute, but I knew we had hit a brick wall. Community disorganization, lack of trust, and political manipulation were the heart of the problem. What could we do?

Meanwhile, I had begun visiting Cacaopera, a town of about 2,000 people eight miles from Gotera. I accompanied the priest every Sunday when he went to say mass. The people in Cacaopera captured my heart from the beginning. Pedro took me to San José, a small camp of about thirty displaced families.

As a visitor described later, "San José makes the camps in Gotera look like the suburbs!" Three rows of tin-roofed modules were spaced about five feet apart. Families of six or eight lived in ten by twelve-foot spaces divided by cornstalk "walls." I learned to sit gingerly in the hammocks concerned that my weight would be too much for the frayed rope or that the rotting two-by-fours would give out.

It wasn't the poor housing that hit me the hardest, though. It was the children. I had seen malnourished children in

Bolivia but nothing like these.

"Please come in," Julia said. Hers was the first *champa* (shack) we came to. "I'm afraid Santos is going to die. Look at him."

She lifted what looked like a bundle of rags from the hammock. Wrapped in the rags was the tiny form of a lethargic baby. I was shocked. He looked like a skeleton.

"He isn't mine," Julia explained. "His mother died right after he was born. She was my sister. His father is so sick and weak that he can't even walk. I'm trying to breast-feed both Santos and my own son, Mario." She held Mario in her other arm. He looked much healthier. "Santos was sickly when he was born and has diarrhea almost constantly. I don't know what to do with him any more."

I looked at Julia. She was distinctively indigenous, with her high cheekbones, wide forehead, dark skin. Her facial features were highlighted by her sunken cheeks and haggard look. She was short, thin, barefoot, wearing a patched cotton dress. Her head didn't even reach my shoulder. How could this frail woman breast-feed two children?

I was shocked by the baby and the worn woman sacrificing her own poorly nourished body to sustain him. There was something compellingly beautiful about Julia—the incongruous beauty of self-sacrificing love in the midst of the ugliness of poverty.

I had mixed feelings as I arranged to start Santos on infant formula. I had little hope he would live. Even if he did survive I wondered about brain damage. But I had to try.

I met other children. There was Isabel with her bloated belly and stick arms. She was struggling to recover from measles. Out of about eighty children, fifteen had already died from a recent measles epidemic. Would she be the next victim of the killer I had always thought of as a "normal" childhood disease?

Then there was Pancha, who reminded me of a fawn with

her big brown eyes. It turned out she was malnourished because she had tuberculosis along with 25 percent of the other children five and under.

The next week I returned to San José with a tape to measure the children's arm circumference—a primitive way of assessing nutritional status. I wanted to weigh all the children but it didn't seem wise to gather a large group together. Cacaopera's recent past was bloody. It had been a risk even for the priest to continue going there for mass. No one knew how far we could go in starting up other programs again. I was new, a lay person, and a health worker—all factors against me in the eyes of the military. I couldn't move too fast.

The displaced, both in Gotera and Cacaopera, complained about the United States Aid for International Development (USAID) work projects. The projects were intended to provide minimal financial assistance to a large number of people by paying them to do community work such as road repair. Men and women signed up for two week stints working for six *colones* a day. Their pay, half of Salvadoran minimum wage, was worth about $1.50. Despite the meager pay, the jobs were in high demand. People were upset that crew foremen signed up friends and family members rather than those who desperately needed the work.

In Cacaopera the accusations were more serious. It was common knowledge that USAID had approved a town water project and the money had been given to the mayor. The water project never materialized. But the mayor suddenly had enough money to buy himself a new truck. People were suspicious and asked me to check into it.

I talked to the USAID director twice. He admitted funds were sometimes mismanaged and said they were looking for a more reliable organization than CONADES (the government Commission for the Displaced), to handle the projects. I wanted to believe mismanagement was the only problem, but the USAID family planning program made me wonder about the real motives behind USAID projects.

It didn't seem right that contraceptives were readily available to women when the hospital didn't even have antibiotics or aspirin. Maureen and I met with the director of the hospital to discuss the fact that so many people were coming to us for medicines.

The director was candid about the problems she faced. "The army base has a better stocked pharmacy than we do but they always use our medicines first. The soldiers get top priority and never pay anything."

She shrugged her shoulders in mute acceptance. The director before her had fled for his life and she had already been threatened. "We also have a problem with doctors siphoning off stock for their private practices. But the main problem is that there's simply not enough money budgeted for health care." She paused. "We receive some medicines from USAID but getting them depends on meeting our quota."

"What quota?" Maureen asked.

"We have to do thirty sterilizations a month to get the medicines," she replied.

I realized that women who refused to go to the hospital because they were harassed probably weren't exaggerating. The quota was divided among nurses and doctors under pressure to bring in women to be sterilized. To see a doctor, patients pass through several points. One nurse registers them, someone else takes their vital signs, another takes them into the examining room. At every step hospital workers try to convince the women to be sterilized.

It was common practice to ask a woman at the peak of labor if she wanted to go through such pain again. If she said "No" they sterilized her.

Occasionally they didn't even get token permission. A woman arrived at the nun's house in tears. She had just given birth to her second child by C-section. When she was re-covering from surgery the doctor asked her if she wanted more children.

"Of course," she responded.

"That's too bad," he said, "because I went ahead and ster-ilized you during the operation."

Another woman had a long history of menstrual prob-lems and vaginal infections. Repeated trips to the hospital outpatient clinic left her no better off than before. Finally a private doctor took an interest in her. Upon examining her he found an IUD obviously placed years earlier. She knew nothing about it. When the doctor went back through her records he found that it had been placed eight years pre-viously without her consent.

Why such an emphasis on family planning? The poor have large families because children are needed to work. High infant mortality rates mean a family needs plenty of children to guarantee that at least some will survive. Popula-tion control studies indicate that when the poor begin to feel a sense of economic security, they voluntarily have fewer children. But family planning programs in El Salvador don't take into account the fact that 2 percent of the population owns 60 percent of the land, leaving the majority of people in an agriculture-based society desperately poor.

The USAID philosophy assumed that there were too many poor people, not that resources were unfairly distrib-uted. Reducing the number of poor people through family planning was one way of relieving the growing pressure for more equitable distribution of resources. Family planning was, therefore, an important counterinsurgency strategy.

In August 1984 we started hearing rumors about a new health program in the camps. Little by little we learned a few details. The name of the program was "Project Hope." It was sponsored by a private organization whose seven million dollar budget for El Salvador was funded by USAID. Their offices were in the U.S. Embassy compound.

Project Hope was interested in coordinating the health programs with us. They called one day when neither Maureen nor I was home. Maureen returned the call the next day. The person she asked for wasn't in but as soon as she said her name the secretary put her right through to the director. It was disconcerting. Why was a big project like that interested in two MCC nurses in Gotera?

We were clear from the start that we didn't want to coordinate with a program linked to questionable USAID policies. When we declined their initiatives, Project Hope workers went to the camps with a list of health promoters we had trained. They offered them a salary of 400 colones a month to work with Project Hope instead of as church volunteers.

Although past broken promises made them leery, the promoters wanted to believe that this time the promises would come true. Each camp was to have its own clinic staffed by nurses. The promoters would do preventive health work and home visits.

Sometime during the months that the Project Hope program was unfolding, I read a document outlining military strategy and humanitarian assistance. According to the paper the military was suspicious of any private organizations which refused to coordinate with government programs. The army considered them the "rearguard of the FMLN rebels" and planned to "neutralize" them.

I was taken aback. That was us. If the document was true, the implications were disturbing. What did it mean to be neutralized? And what was wrong with keeping our church programs separate from the government ones?

I began hearing terms like "winning hearts and minds," "pacification" programs, "low intensity conflict," and "draining the sea to kill the fish." A military official graphically explained the concept of draining the sea to kill the fish. He took a fish bowl to a meeting with a group of people who had chosen to stay in their homes in the countryside.

"You are the sea," he told them. "And the fish are the subversives. Without the water the fish die." He poured the water on the ground. "That's why if you stay here we might have to do what we did in Mozote." He was referring to the massacre in which the army killed over 900 people.

The army drove rural peasants to Gotera by threats, massacres, and bombs. Once in Gotera the pacification started. Instead of being the "bad guys" who killed civilians, the army attempted to portray itself as the "good guys" who gave the people food and medicine. I realized that people controlled by terror are easily pacified. Wanting to believe that the killers have changed, they cling to any indication which points in that direction.

The International Red Cross was responsible for distributing food in Cacaopera. But for several months in a row the colonel denied permission for their trucks of food to pass. Just when people were getting desperate, the army arrived and gave a few pounds of corn and beans to each family. During my next visit I heard nothing but praise for the colonel's kindness. People were too scared to let themselves think about the fact that the colonel created the very need he then met with less than half the rations they would have received from the Red Cross.

Health care was another aspect of the pacification programs. The army periodically initiated what it called civic action campaigns. Several huge troop carrier trucks would roar into a village. Soldiers would distribute a few pounds of beans or rice to people, literally throwing the rations off the trucks into the hands of the pushing, shoving crowd. Sometimes they brought clowns or the army band to create a festive atmosphere. Doctors from the local public hospital were required to help with the campaigns.

One particular experience revealed that the army's motives were more to win people's favor than to improve the health of the poor. The doctor from the army base announced that all doctors at the hospital were to go with him the following day.

One doctor protested. "What about the patients in the hospital?" she asked. "We attend over 300 outpatients a day."

"You can stay if you want," was the icy reply.

The doctor stayed and was later forced to leave the country because of threats.

The doctors who went were disgusted. "We were 'under orders' to use the medicines available," one explained. "Since the only medicine available was for intestinal parasites, that's what we had to give no matter what the disease."

The colonel frequently tried to make a public link between the military and the church. On "Soldiers' Day" the colonel would invite priests to say mass for the troops. And on special occasions the priests would be asked to join government and military officials for speeches on the main platform. The priests would think up excuses to refuse since they did not want to legitimize a military and government structure responsible for so many abuses.

Although I was used to the priests being asked to identify themselves with the military, I was surprised when Maureen and I received an unexpected invitation. At about 7:00 p.m. one evening there was a knock on our door. There stood an American military adviser and four civilians, obviously Americans as well. They said they had come to visit so we invited them in. The adviser introduced himself. He was an evangelical Christian from a Hispanic family and had a degree in psychology. His friends were health workers from an evangelical group called "Para Vida" which means "For Life."

The adviser took control of the conversation, talking freely of his hopes to "Christianize" the army. He spoke of poor peasant conscripts whom he wanted to help learn to read.

He talked about the human rights abuses and his desire to make the war more humane.

Then he got on the subjection of corruption. Twice he blurted out, "What this country needs is a REVOLUTION!" But he caught himself, saying, "But we're not going to let it happen. We're going to change things slowly by flooding El Salvador with American influence."

Maureen and I were taken aback by his outbursts. I couldn't believe an American officer with a psychology degree had accidentally gotten carried away demanding a revolution. Was he trying to get a reaction out of us? But why?

After a while the reason for the visit became clear. The four health workers were being hosted by the army to do a health campaign in the camps. They were going to visit each camp and hand out medicines. They wanted us to translate.

We tried to explain that we focused our work on training and prevention in the countryside where no services were available. Spending a day giving out medicines in the camps wouldn't solve long-term problems. I had learned that lesson well with the El Tiangue latrines.

"Maybe not," one visitor responded. "But in the last camp we visited we saved the life of a man who would have died of pneumonia if we hadn't arrived when we did. It was God's timing. God led us to be there right at that moment."

He was obviously sincere. He felt good about saving one life because he wasn't asking why the man had to live in a camp. I wished I could help him understand that U.S. government support for the Salvadoran military had helped create the conditions that now demanded his attention.

I didn't know how to respond, especially with the adviser there. How could I explain that I thought health work was being manipulated, that the army was trying to use us to promote its image in the camps? If the military cared so much about poor, sick people, why did they make it so hard for us to work out in the countryside where health work was really needed? Why did they cut off medical services in rural areas and promote them in Gotera? They were using medicines like a carrot on a stick to get people to live where they wanted them to live. And what about saving lives? Did the possibility of saving one life make it worth joining hands with killers of thousands?

We tried to raise the issues but our different perspectives kept us from communicating. Finally one visitor said, "I don't understand what you are saying, but I'll pray for wisdom." We prayed together and they left. What a diverse group, each of us sincerely following convictions we felt were inspired by God. How could we come out at such different places?

During the first few months of 1985 my questions about what it meant to be neutralized were answered. The health workers we had trained began working with Project Hope. Clinics were under construction in the camps and nutrition centers were being built. The glittering promises successfully undermined our less glamorous efforts at grassroots empowerment. There was no reason for us to stay and compete. We had been neutralized.

In a year the people were begging us to work in the camps again. The clinics didn't have medicines. The nurses scolded them. The health promoters had lost their sense of sacrifice and service once they began working for salaries. But by that time we were busy with programs in the countryside.

Several years later, I read several documents on low intensity conflict which helped clarify my experience in Gotera. An internal U.S. military document described the U.S. advisers' perspective on El Salvador. It said, "We view El Salvador as providing fertile ground—until now largely uncultivated—for teaching Americans how to fight small wars."[2] I was taken aback by the assumption that the U.S. was literally at war in El Salvador. "We were at war. We had been at war—at least since 1981."[3]

Low-intensity conflict (LIC) was the new strategy for fighting small wars. The Navy referred to LIC as "violent peace."[4] The idea was to fight communism by waging psychological warfare, not by committing U.S. troops to battle. Humanitarian aid was a key component.

In his book *War Against the Poor, Low-Intensity Conflict and the Christian Faith*, Jack Nelson-Pallmeyer quotes a U.S. general who said, " 'Humanitarian assistance is a fundamental Department of Defense mission in low-intensity conflict.' It is an 'integral part of military operations.' "[5] Our wariness of becoming involved in government humanitarian aid programs was well founded.

6

Learning to Live Amidst Suffering

It wasn't hard to let go of our work in the camps once Project Hope took over, because I was already involved in Cacaopera. About two-thirds of the people originally from Cacaopera left in the early years of the war.

The displacement followed a general pattern. People from town who had money went to San Salvador or to the U.S. Others, including some of the wealthier people from outlying villages, went to Gotera. The poorest people from the villages were split. Some stayed in their homes, others fled to the refugee camp of Colomancagua, and the rest went to Cacaopera. Generally the poorest people from indigenous background settled in Cacaopera.

Mario taught me the history of the indigenous people. Although not indigenous himself, he took great interest in their cause. As director of Cacaopera's "House of History and Culture," he had many opportunities to promote the dignity of the once-proud Mayans.

Mario explained that when the Spanish Conquerors invaded El Salvador in 1524, they found the Indians living in community doing cooperative farming. It took fifteen years for the Spaniards to conquer the Indians. They eventually destroyed the Indian way of life, taking over community property and forcing them to cultivate indigo on large plantations.

In 1841, El Salvador became a republic. At the same time, the demand for indigo decreased and coffee production took its place. More of the best land was expropriated for coffee, so the landowners got richer while the poor got poorer.

Then the Great Depression hit. Coffee prices fell, leaving the workers destitute. On January 22, 1932, a popular insurrection broke out and the peasants, mostly indigenous, killed thirty-five civilians and 100 soldiers. The army retaliated by massacring 30,000 peasants over a period of three weeks. Being indigenous became a stigma. People stopped speaking their native language or wearing their traditional dress, fearful that they too would be killed.

Still some of the older women in Cacaopera continued to dress in distinctively indigenous ways. They pulled their long hair back in braids and wore full skirted, pleated cotton dresses. One man in Cacaopera could speak a little *Nahuat*, the language of that area, but it was hard to convince him to do so unless he was drunk.

The recent history of Cacaopera was also tragic. Sister Anselma's account of what took place on Ash Wednesday 1983 is one of many similar stories.

> It was Ash Wednesday and Father Gerry and I had been to Cacaopera for Mass. Apparently after we left, the National Guard arrested seven people. They arrested Julio, the catechist; his wife, Gumercinda; and Agustina, his sister. Then there was Mariá Apolonia who had no direct connection with the others except she was also poor and came from Calavera, one of the outlying villages. The other three men were from a wealthy family and well-known in the town.
>
> After we heard the news Thursday morning, Nelson, a

seminarian, and I went to Cacaopera. We parked the car and walked through town. I don't think I'll ever forget that walk because, as we passed by, the doors opened and people started joining us. It was as if they were afraid to go out until they saw somebody else. By the time we got to the clinic there must have been 100 people.

We went in and an old man was there sewing up grain sacks. He had gathered pieces of the bodies which had been hacked to bits with machetes and sewed them into sacks for burial.

I was crying too hard to pray, so Nelson said some prayers. Then we all went to the cemetery where Apolonia was being buried and prayed there, too. After that people began searching for the bodies of the men. There had been shooting at 9:00 p.m. the night before so we thought the men had been killed as well.

Not having found a trace of the men, we went to the National Guard and the civil defense. Both groups denied knowing anything about the murders.

Then I remembered that the American ambassador, Dean Hinton, was going to be in Gotera. Maybe he could use his influence to find the men. Nelson and I jumped in the car and hurried to Gotera, hoping to catch him. We called him and he agreed to see us. I was crying so hard I could hardly talk. I told him about the three bodies macheteed to bits and said I wanted to know what had happened to the men.

The ambassador told us that, if the U.S. had been training the Salvadoran troops, those kind of problems wouldn't be happening. He agreed to look into it. The only result of our talk was that the head of the National Guard in Cacaopera was transferred to Gotera. A week later he was in a jeep with three other guardsman, all drunk. They drove into a post just outside of town and were killed. That was the end of the inquiry.

We found out what had happened from Julio. The three men from the wealthy family had been released right away because so many people from town knew them and spoke up for them. They were let out at about 7:00 p.m. and went straight home to their village. No one from town realized they had been freed.

Julio was the only man left. His wife had managed to loosen the cords around his hands but he acted as if they were securely tied.

They were all taken to a field. The guardsmen killed the women first. As they were killing Apolonia, one of them asked the man guarding Julio to shine his flashlight because he couldn't see. The guard stepped over with the flashlight.

In that instant Julio slipped his hands out of the cords, took off his shirt, and threw it into the air as he ran in the opposite direction. The guards shot at the shirt and Julio escaped unharmed.

That story introduced me to many issues. Catechists targeted. Poor women hacked to death for no reason. Men released because of money and prestige. Lying guardsmen. The courage of people who buried the bodies once they knew they weren't alone. The ambassador's recognition that the recipients of U.S. funds were responsible for atrocities and his inability or unwillingness to do anything about it. Gumercinda's self-sacrifice and Julio's creativity in planning his escape. I came to recognize the same themes in story after story.

The stories I heard were so horrible that I dealt with them emotionally by trying to make the time gap longer than it actually was. *Maybe atrocities happened in 1980 and 1981 but this is 1984. Things have changed,* I unconsciously thought to myself. An occasional glimpse of someone's fear, however, forced me back to reality. It takes more than two or three years to work through the terror of repression.

Ana reminded me of that truth. One day I was sitting in her house visiting. We had been working together for about six months but our relationship had been superficial. It takes a long time to build trust. This time the conversation became serious. She lowered her voice until I had to strain to hear her.

We were alone in the house but she looked around anyway to see if anyone was near. "My husband is related to Father Octavio," she whispered. (Father Octavio Ortiz was killed by the military in 1979.) "He grew up here. The rest of his relatives fled after he was killed."

She abruptly stood up and looked out the door. Then she pulled her Bible from the shelf and carefully leafed through the pages until she found a small card. She handed it to me. It was a picture of Father Octavio with a Bible verse.

"These were handed out at his funeral," she said. "Afterwards anyone caught with it was tortured and killed so I buried mine."

I shuddered as I felt her fear about something that seemed so harmless to me. Why should she be scared to admit that she was related to Father Octavio? Was that a crime? Ana knew better than I did, however, that repression needs no crime.

Another incident while I was in Cacaopera destroyed my naive assumptions that the atrocities were past. I was riding back to Gotera with the clinic health team. The doctor had an armadillo tied up on the floor.

"I had a patient today who didn't even have the .20 fee for the medical exam. So his father offered me this armadillo." He was obviously pleased at the exchange.

Later I learned that the father had been captured by soldiers as he left the clinic. Someone had pointed him out as a guerrilla sympathizer. They took him and the ten-year-old boy to the cemetery. But the father managed to get his hands loose and took off running while his guards were occupied. It never occurred to him that they would harm the boy. He was wrong. Angry that he had escaped, the soldiers killed the boy and left his decapitated body in the cemetery.

That incident is connected with an experience that helped me begin to understand fear personally. We were in the middle of a church service in Cacaopera when shooting started. It sounded as if it was coming from the cemetery. Several men closed the heavy wooden church doors. The shooting came closer. I was glad to be in the church with its thick adobe walls.

Then the shots echoed so close that I wondered if they were hitting the building. We moved quickly but calmly away from the center to the safety of the walls. Huddled on the floor, we began reciting repetitive prayers. The rise and fall of the familiar words had a soothing effect. I was impressed with how calm people were, even the children.

When the shooting stopped and the service resumed, Sister Anselma told about the boy who had been decapitated. "The soldiers who killed him aren't the only ones responsible for his death," she said. Her voice trembled with emotion and conviction. "Whoever falsely denounced the father as a guerrilla sympathizer is equally responsible."

I was listening intently when I realized that a soldier was standing behind Anselma on the altar. My chest tightened in horror and my pulse began to race. She didn't know he was behind her. What if she says more against the military? Should I try to warn her?

I looked at the soldier. His face was painted camouflage green. A red bandana was tied around his head. He held his M-16 menacingly, ready to shoot at the slightest provocation. Images of Archbishop Oscar Romero (shot while presiding over mass) haunted my mind. I feared for Anselma's life.

Several more soldiers entered and sauntered down the aisles. At least Anselma knew now that they were listening. They searched the faces of the congregation as if to dare anyone to challenge their authority. Their eyes peered grotesquely from their painted faces. Accusing. Threatening.

I mirrored the indifferent faces of those around me. Mask in place, I steeled my heart and looked straight ahead like everyone else.

Anselma continued. "I repeat: whoever denounced the father is equally responsible for the boy's death. The tongue is a vicious weapon. Christians must learn to control their tongues." She stepped down from the podium and we sang the closing song.

The more I learned about Cacaopera and the more I experienced during my visits, the more strongly I felt drawn to work there. I was frustrated just going with the priest on Sunday mornings, so I started going with the mobile health team from the hospital. A doctor and two public health nurses attended the clinic twice a week.

While they saw patients I visited San José. I began working with the nine most severely malnourished children. I weighed them twice a month and taught the mothers to make a high protein, high calorie milk and oil mixture.

I worked intensely with little Santos, the malnourished baby I encountered on my first visit. He was four months old and weighed seven pounds. He would start to gain a little when another bout of diarrhea would send his weight plummeting again. I never knew when I left if he would be alive when I returned. He proved himself a fighter, though. By the time he was two years old he was as healthy as any other child in the camps.

I learned more about Santos' family history. His father, Felicito, had tuberculosis. He had been in treatment but quit because he didn't have money for bus fare to the treatment center. Santos' mother died after he was born. It sounded as if she had T.B. as well. I learned from the clinic health team that Cacaopera had long been a focal point for T.B. It was spreading because of the poor living conditions in the camp.

The year before, the health team and the parish had coordinated an effort to send a number of people in for chest X rays. Those with positive results started a yearlong course of treatment but lack of follow-up meant that the majority never finished. Not finishing T.B. treatment can result in the development of strains resistant to medication.

Undaunted by previous failed attempts to deal with the T.B. problem, I threw myself into establishing a treatment program. I read about T.B., wrote letters, met with the clinic team, made plans with the hospital in Gotera, visited the regional T.B. treatment center in San Miguel, and talked with ministry of health officials. I came up with a realistic plan for screening and treatment that would involve coordination between the clinics and hospitals.

The initial response of those involved was positive. But when I tried to move past the planning stages, obstacles emerged. The hospital didn't have x-ray film. The ministry of health didn't have enough medication. There was infighting between regional offices. The clinic doctor was finishing his required year and there was no guarantee that he would be replaced. The clinic was even in danger of being closed.

All plans for a T.B. program fell through. I was discouraged and angry as I realized that poor people in Cacaopera were not a priority.

The next months were difficult. When we first arrived, it seemed as if there were many opportunities to work. Time confirmed the tremendous health needs but also proved there were walls behind the open doors. I was frustrated. We were doing nothing more than putting bandage strips on a sieve.

The MCC team had many long discussions about our work. We felt God challenging us to respond to suffering people no matter who they were or what they believed. It wasn't right to allow the government to define where, how, and with whom we worked.

According to the government's definition of neutrality, I could give out medicines to the displaced in Gotera but I couldn't deal with the roots of the health problems. Nor could I work with people who had chosen to stay in their homes in the countryside without being accused of making a political commitment to the FMLN. We believed that Christians need to be present on both sides of any conflict, giving priority to suffering people regardless of their political persuasion.

Since it seemed our work in Gotera wasn't going anywhere, I volunteered to help investigate other potential areas. I was convinced this was right and was determined to do it even if I was afraid of the consequences.

I experienced God at that point as a God of demands. Luke 12:48 felt like a threat. "From anyone who has been given much, much will be demanded, and from the one who has been entrusted with much, much more will be asked." I had been given much, so I took the weight of the demands on myself.

Then I got hepatitis. In theory I wanted to do what I thought was right. But it was a relief to have a good excuse for not doing it. I was vaguely depressed during that time, as my heart, head, and body battled with each other over right and wrong.

The MCC unit struggled as well. We could discuss life and death issues and easily reach consensus. How ironic, then, that it would take forty-five minutes of talking in circles to decide what movie to see or where we would eat when we were together for our monthly meetings.

But the big issue we discussed for months was whether or not it was right to be hiring someone to wash the sheets and towels in our house in the capital. Relationships at times were tense and strained. We needed each other so badly. We were so determined to do what was right. We wanted so much to be community. But the pressure was too much. Where was the energy to support others, when individually we were barely surviving?

During that time Maureen had a timely visit from a close friend who was a trained therapist. After observing our group dynamics, she said she would either have to help us or leave during our discussions, because she couldn't stand watching us.

We gladly accepted her help. She met with us several times. This didn't solve our problems but did provide some valuable tools. We were able to look at ourselves and laugh. We also took the Myers-Briggs Personality tests, which helped us understand that we all had different ways of perceiving and responding to the world. No one was purposefully trying to be difficult.

Blake, our spontaneous, extroverted director, would bring up a matter to be discussed with the group. We would make a decision and invariably the next day Ron or I thought of another point that should have been considered. Blake would understandably get frustrated. Why hadn't we brought it up during the discussion before the decision was made? We learned that Ron and I were introverted and processed ideas internally instead of verbally with the group. We needed a chance to think before forming opinions.

The team looked at ways to make our meetings more beneficial. I felt embraced and accepted when I realized the others valued my opinions enough to structure meetings in a way that allowed me to participate fully. Even though it took effort given his spontaneous character, Blake would try to let me know beforehand what issues we were going to discuss. Sometimes we would talk about a topic, then take a few minutes to think about it individually before making a decision.

We learned valuable lessons through our struggles. We saw how we were displacing stress and tension. Small incidents were blown out of proportion as a stress reaction to major issues. We came to a better understanding of ourselves as individuals—and what that meant for group dynamics. And we learned ways of structuring our time together so it was both more restful and productive.

After reevaluating our work, we decided I should focus

more time and energy in Cacaopera. I began assessing how I could expand my work there. What would the military let me get away with? Where was "the line"? What would be the consequences if I went too far? I was afraid.

We all agreed that it wasn't ideal for me to be going there alone, but I didn't see any other alternatives. In January 1985 I started spending several nights a week in Cacaopera.

I stayed in the convent behind the church. The convent consisted of two bare rooms with a table and shelves. It had adobe walls and a tile roof. Five displaced families had their shacks built next to it so I had close neighbors.

My neighbors were so near that they constantly reminded me of my affluence. I bought some bread one afternoon, but when I got home I realized that it was already old and a little moldy. It sat for a few days before I put it in a plastic bowl of garbage along with some onion skins and mango peels. Since everybody else gives their garbage to the pigs, I did the same. As I was throwing it out, however, I noticed that one woman was watching me. I glanced over my shoulder just in time to see her rescue the bread and onion skins from the pig who was already nosing it. Later the same day, I saw her give three big tortillas to a retarded woman who survives begging for food.

From then on I was faced with a garbage dilemma. Lifestyle decisions were no longer theoretical. I lived with people who were directly affected by my choices. What should I do with moldy bread? Eat it myself? Throw it out in secret? Offer it to my neighbors—"Here, this isn't good enough for me, but I thought you might like it"?

Then there was my trash. Children would gather around to rescue precious treasures before I burned them. I found myself explaining that the only reason I was burning the plastic bag was because it had a big hole and that I tried not to waste paper but had to write lots of reports. "Yes, you can take the paper home. You're right. It makes much better toilet paper than corncobs and leaves." I even sneaked my garbage back to Gotera a few times just so I could throw it out anonymously in peace.

I remained concerned about the many suspected T.B. cases I encountered. The T.B. program at that point consisted of giving Felicito bus fare for his monthly appointment in San Miguel. It was encouraging to see his improvement, and people in the camp noted how much better he was. Another man had T.B. symptoms. Since he was afraid to go to San Miguel alone, it occurred to me he could go with Felicito—who was thrilled to help someone else.

And so over the next year a small but solid T.B. program began to take shape. As members of the parish health team, we became advocates for the poor who often get lost in the public health care system. We helped with logistics and sometimes supplied medicines or x-ray film. But the program depended on the poor helping each other.

I had never visited the villages outside of Cacaopera, so when some men interested in health classes in Tierra Blanca invited me to visit, I decided to go. It was exhilarating to walk in the countryside, to breathe the fresh air, and to see the mountains.

I enjoyed visiting people in their homes. It gave me an idea of what the displaced had left in exchange for the dirty, crowded camps. The village was only a forty-five minute walk away and it felt so easy to go there. What was the big deal? Why did people with more experience think it was such a security risk?

It took about two weeks to feel the consequences of my visit. I was amazed at the number of comments people made. They weren't necessarily negative, but everyone in town knew I had walked to Tierra Blanca.

I soon learned that town people weren't the only ones aware of my visit. Juan pulled me aside Sunday after mass. "The soldiers came through Tierra Blanca the other day," he said in a low voice. "They asked who you were and what you were doing there. I told them you worked with the church giving health classes. They asked a few more questions, then said it was okay as long as we didn't talk about the war or politics."

The thrill of my visit was shattered by the reality of being watched. It seemed so natural to be in Tierra Blanca. I had felt relaxed and at peace. But I realized my feelings were misguided. I could only feel that way as long as I was naive. Once I knew that under the tranquil surface was a bubbling layer of doubt and suspicion, I could never quite relax again.

Had I made a mistake? Had I gone too far, too fast? What would be the consequences for the people in the health class? After consulting with a number of people, we decided that it was all right to keep going to Tierra Blanca since the soldiers knew anyhow, but it was better not to go to other villages.

After that I never walked out of Cacaopera without evaluating first. Soldiers were in the area. Did that mean it was best not to go this time? Or mortars had fallen the night before. Would the army be suspicious if I went the next day? I felt tense as I struggled to be prudent but not intimidated.

In the midst of the fear and tension another powerful emotion burst forth. I fell in love! The friendship between another volunteer and me blossomed into a romance. Our relationship developed at the same time I was questioning my commitment to El Salvador. I was feeling insecure about my work and wasn't sure where I fit in the parish. I needed someone to believe in me when I was having trouble believing in myself.

April was the crisis point. I knew I needed a home, which meant I either had to go back to the U.S. or put my roots down where I was.

I can't recall what made me finally rent a house in Cacaopera and make that my home. Maybe I was beginning to realize that I was using our relationship as a convenient excuse to escape a situation that seemed to be more than I could handle. Anyway, I chose to give Cacaopera another chance. My friend and I mutually decided to end our romantic involvement. When his term ended soon afterward, we parted on good terms.

The relationship left a lasting impression as I allowed myself to accept my need for intimacy. Having that need met for a time helped me begin searching for committed relationships that would provide intimacy and security apart from romantic involvement.

My concept of security was being redefined during those months as well. I was faced head on with my limitations and felt God's love for me anyway. I realized that clearcut definitions of right or wrong had more to do with my need for structure than with God's character. If I trusted the Spirit of God within me I would be able to discern truth in a given situation without legalistically following the letter of the law.

Carmen, a Salvadoran working with the parish health team, and Blake were helping me move into my newly rented house when the army arrested us. The experience confirmed my recent decision to stay.

7

Under Arrest

Friday. May 10, 1985. 5:30 p.m. San Salvador, El Salvador. I look around my cell. Two beds, bare walls, a reasonably clean toilet. A few rays of light filter down from a narrow row of slats above my bed. I struggle to glimpse the sky. Standing on my tiptoes I can see a square inch. I'm reassured. I check my watch. *At least I won't lose my sense of time*, I think.

A uniformed man enters and takes inventory of everything in my purse. "For safe keeping," he says. He requests my watch. I feel my control slipping away. I'm scared.

The first indication of trouble came on Thursday morning. I was in Cacaopera moving into my new house. Blake (MCC volunteer) and Carmen (a Salvadoran co-worker) were helping me move when a church member arrived to warn us that the soldiers had questioned her about me.

She repeated some of their questions. "What does she do? Why is she here? Why is she moving into a house? Is she North American?"

A few hours later soldiers interrupted our lunch. One came in and sat down while several others surrounded the house. The soldier in charge checked our identification papers and asked questions about our work. As he left, he said they might be back.

We finished lunch, decided to cancel a health class in a neighboring village, and began working in the garden. At 2:00 p.m. the soldiers entered the house unannounced. I was annoyed. They said that the lieutenant wanted to talk to us and we were to go with them.

We took our time preparing to leave. I was relieved that Blake was along but concerned about Carmen since the army tends to respect foreigners and mistreat Salvadorans. We were escorted up the hill outside of town with two soldiers in front and two in back. I made a point of greeting everyone I saw, hoping they would be suspicious of the soldiers accompanying us.

The lieutenant was nonchalantly sprawled on the grass when we arrived. He gave an order to send a radio message, then turned to us. I idly wondered if we were the subject of the message. He requested our documents, asking if we knew the expiration dates. His questions seemed more like chitchat than an interrogation.

Rain started sprinkling and we were taken to a nearby house. Ten minutes later we heard a helicopter and a soldier came to get us.

The lieutenant informed us we were being taken to the military barracks in San Francisco Gotera. "I hope it's no trouble. You don't have plans this afternoon, do you? Don't worry, we'll bring you right back."

His politeness struck me as insincere. What was going on? We climbed into the helicopter and took off. The recent spring rains had infused the countryside with new life. My mind couldn't comprehend that the splendid view was made possible by an instrument of war, that the gunner at my side was poised to kill. We quickly approached Gotera and passed over the MCC house. I wondered what my co-worker, Maureen, was doing.

A jeep was waiting for us when we arrived at Gotera. We drove past the priest's house to the barracks. I searched for a familiar face along the road but saw no one. We waited just inside the entrance of the barracks for an hour and a half. Looking out the gate I saw the plaza I passed every time I visited the priests.

Everything was familiar. So why did looking from the barracks out to the plaza seem so different than looking from the plaza toward the barracks? Was it because I felt trapped? Or maybe it was being in the shadow of a huge mural of a skull and cross bones painted on the barracks wall.

My thoughts were interrupted by the church bells. Time for 4:00 p.m. mass. Padre Alfredo was only several hundred yards away. If he only knew.

Meanwhile, several officers questioned us. "Why do you work in Cacaopera when there are plenty of displaced people in Gotera?" one of them asked.

I responded that since lots of institutions worked in Gotera and no one was helping in Cacaopera, we decided we were needed most in Cacaopera. We asked why we had been taken and requested to see someone in charge.

One officer replied that we were in a conflictive zone without permission from the colonel.

"We work with the parish," Blake explained. "The parish team informs each new colonel about the work we do but we never ask for military permission to work within our parish. You can call the priests if you want to clarify our position."

"We don't trust them."

"Then call the nuns," Blake said.

"We trust them even less," was the curt reply.

An hour later we were loaded into a minibus headed for the regional military headquarters in San Miguel. Eight soldiers accompanied us, each armed with M-16's and grenades dangling from shoulder straps.

We drove within sight of the priests' house, the nuns' house, and the old convent where Maureen and I lived. I kept my eyes glued to the window hoping to see someone from the parish team. We stopped to get gas, turned, and came back the same route to pick up another soldier. I was sure that with a second chance I would see someone I knew. I was disappointed.

We arrived in San Miguel just in time for the 6:00 p.m. rendition of the national anthem. No one indicated they were expecting us. The soldiers from Gotera went back and we were left sitting outside unattended. A soldier asked whom we had come to visit. I began to relax. *It can't be very serious if they treat us like this*, I thought.

As it began to get dark we were invited into the waiting room. We asked the officer why we had been taken. He didn't seem to know. We requested to see someone in charge and make a phone call. Both requests were denied. Time passed slowly. We played games with Blake's watch, glad at least that we were all three together.

I observed the soldiers. They were bored and passing time just like us. There was a clear pecking order among them. Respect for higher rank was based on fear. But it was Mother's Day; the phone was busy as the men called their wives and mothers to express their love and appreciation.

We were clearly treated as a special case. When we were hungry, a soldier was sent to buy whatever we wanted— with our money, of course. Thursday evening we dined on hamburgers and french fries. When I asked where we were to sleep they sent for mattresses which we laid on the waiting room floor.

Friday morning the security was still relaxed. We insisted on seeing someone in charge but were put off. There was talk of turning us over to the U.S. embassy in the capital. We sat outside playing word games, then moved further away from the building under a tree.

It was midmorning when a delegate from the International Red Cross arrived. She knew we had been captured but was surprised to see us in San Miguel. We barely had a chance to exchange greetings when an officer whisked her away. It was then politely suggested that we would be more comfortable inside the building. Entering the waiting room once again, we sat down on a bench against the far wall. Soldiers barricaded the entrance with another bench.

I was excited to see the Red Cross delegate and expected to be released to her custody. We had a lively discussion about how we could celebrate our arrival back to Gotera exactly twenty-four hours after we were captured. I tried to ignore the gnawing doubt that we might not be set free.

Carmen and I were pacing back and forth to stretch our legs when we saw the Red Cross delegate being escorted to her car. She looked back toward where we were held, craning her neck in an effort to see if we were still there. My heart sank. They weren't going to release us after all. Someone had plans for us. It wasn't just a mistake. We sat in uneasy silence as efforts to find a helicopter to transfer us intensified.

At 3:00 p.m. we were taken by helicopter to the airport in San Miguel. There we waited an hour for the arrival of a DC-3 military transport plane. More people wanted to go than the plane could take but, as prisoners, we were given first priority.

During the twenty-five-minute flight Blake and I discussed our strategy for answering questions. It seemed possible we would be forced to leave the country. I realized how much I wanted to stay. But my life would go on. I became increasingly concerned about Carmen. As a Salvadoran she wasn't protected by international publicity like we were.

We landed at the airport we use when we take the air taxi from San Miguel. The familiar sights reminded me of the many times I had chosen to go there. This time was different. I had not chosen to come. I was a prisoner with no control. Reality began to sink in.

Waiting at the airport I saw a Treasury policeman who looked like Darth Vader in his shiny black helmet and knee-high black boots. Knowing their reputation for ruthlessness, I was relieved that we were in the hands of the army. A short time later a group of uniformed men entered. They introduced themselves as being from the Treasury police. They would be taking us to their headquarters. My pulse quickened.

We climbed into a custom-made van with shag carpet, plush seats, bullet-proof glass, dark windows. It looked worn from use. I had read about these death squad vans. I wondered how many people had been beaten where my feet now rested. Detached, I wondered how they cleaned the blood off the shag carpet.

At the police headquarters we were taken to the employee's lounge. *Maybe it won't be so bad after all*, I thought to myself.

Blake asked the lieutenant how long we would be held.

"Maybe three hours or six hours. Or it could be a day or two or three."

What did they want with us? After a few minutes we were told we would be separated. They took Carmen first. I prayed for her protection. Then I was taken by car to another building. It was late Friday afternoon. We had been prisoners for over twenty-four hours.

A nurse came to my cell to make sure I was okay. He offered me Valium, a tranquilizer, and said he would come back every day. Why did he think I might need a tranquilizer? I desperately wanted to assure him that he wouldn't find me the next day. After all, I was getting out soon, wasn't I?

A man who turned out to be my interrogator took my purse and watch. It reminded me of checking into a hospital. Impersonal. Dehumanizing. The machine runs like clockwork, swallowing up individuals and spitting out prisoners.

I tried to concentrate on whatever would occupy my

mind. I didn't know how long I would be alone with nothing to do. When the national anthem started I knew it was 6:00 p.m. I decided that the band in Gotera played far better than this one. I was brought supper—beans, rice, tortillas, and plantains. I was surprised that I was able to eat. I tried to chew each bite thirty times before I swallowed. I prayed.

Soon after supper the vice-consul from the U.S. Embassy came and explained that I was charged with teaching Marxist doctrine. The accusation struck me as absurd. I didn't know anything about Marxism. Were they referring to my health and Bible classes?

"But it's no problem. You'll be out tonight."

His boisterous voice cut through my thoughts. I wanted to think it would be that easy. But I was doubtful since it was after working hours on a Friday evening. He went on to say how much the Treasury police had changed and that he had complete confidence in them.

I didn't believe him. I was reassured, however, to know that the MCC volunteers had contacted him. Another kind of machine was set in motion. This one was working for my good. My heart went out to prisoners who feel forgotten and abandoned. I asked the embassy official to make sure he saw Carmen. He wouldn't promise.

The interrogation began as soon as he left. My interrogator was about twenty-five and dressed in a military uniform. He had short black hair, a moustache, and a mole in the middle of his chin. He looked like any young man one might meet on the street. He was well trained in the techniques of interrogation. Sometimes he was friendly and agreeable, leading me on with a nod and a smile. But in an instant his manner would become cold and hard.

Sometimes he paced the floor as he asked a question slowly and deliberately. Then he would whirl around sticking his face close to mine, his eyes penetrating as he awaited my response.

"What is Marx's first name? Tell me everything you know about Marxism. What Bible verse did Marx use to mislead the working class in London?"

Trying to regain at least a semblance of control, I said I didn't know what verse Marx used and asked him to tell me.

I caught him off guard. "I . . . I don't know the exact verse," he stumbled. "But Marx used the Bible to make people dissatisfied with the class system." Gaining confidence, he continued. "Marx manipulated the Bible. He taught that it wasn't God's will for some to be rich and others poor. Of course, God loves everyone equally but that doesn't mean that some won't have more than others."

The interrogation continued. "What do you teach in your Bible classes? Why do you talk about the poor working together? How could your lessons be misunderstood? When did you give the political talks? Why do you teach the poor that God loves them?"

The reason for the last question puzzled me. What was he driving at? "I teach the poor that God loves them because it's true," I responded simply.

The questions went on. "What is Lenin's first name? Federico? Vladimir? Distinguish between Marxism, Communism, Leninism, and Socialism."

The questions had me stumped. I didn't bother trying to think up answers but said repeatedly that I didn't know.

"When did you give the political talks? We have proof that you give them so why don't you just admit it? Why do you give Bible classes on working together?"

I lost all sense of time.

"When did you first enter the country? How did you enter? Why did you come by land? Where did you go first? Who is the first person you talked to? When did you go to Gotera?"

The questions kept coming. I felt bombarded. I just wanted him to go away.

Finally he sat down and pushed a piece of paper toward me. "It would be much easier for you to write the places and dates of your political talks," he said. "I don't want to have to hurt you or force you out of the country but if you can't remember I'll have to help you."

I was stunned. Had I misunderstood or was he actually threatening me?

"I'll be back soon to see if you've remembered," he promised on his way out the door.

I lay on the bed, my heart thumping. I rationalized that it would be counterproductive to injure a North American. They wouldn't dare. It would be bad publicity. After all, the U.S. government gives El Salvador over a million dollars a day. They wouldn't put that in jeopardy by harming a U.S. citizen.

But a shadow of doubt remained. I knew Salvadoran interrogators were trained in torture techniques. I prayed for presence of mind. I asked God's protection for Carmen and mercy for the many Salvadorans who were more than just threatened with torture.

Although I was exhausted from not having slept the night before, I couldn't quiet my reeling mind. What could I tell him to get him off my back? I mentally reviewed my classes with the displaced people. There was the class on 1 Peter 2 where we discussed what it meant to be living stones built up into a spiritual temple. That was the beginning of the nutrition program. The verses inspired them to work together to face the malnutrition problem in the camp.

Then there was the class about Nehemiah rebuilding the wall of Jerusalem. They could really identify with that one since they were displaced like Nehemiah. We had a good discussion about the obstacles Nehemiah faced and the obstacles they faced trying to help the children.

But I had already explained the Bible studies. What more could I say? My interrogator had such power over me. I wanted to satisfy him so he would leave me alone. I began to understand why the oppressed try so hard to please their oppressors.

When I heard the key turn in the door I bolted, my heart pounding, my hands sweaty. He was coming back to see if I remembered about the political talks! But it was just the guard checking. The same thing happened at least four more times. I was relieved when morning finally came.

Saturday morning the interrogation started again. It was the same interrogator but this time he was dressed in civilian clothes. He made no reference to the night before. For the first several hours he was concerned with filling out file forms—name, age, birthday, father's name, high school, college, and on and on and on. Since he couldn't understand the English names he had me write them down.

The embassy official interrupted one session. But this time he wasn't so optimistic about our release. He offered to bring me a change of clothes and some books. I had the impression that it might be several more days. Later I learned that he had told the MCCers that it could be up to fifteen days. I was frustrated that he hadn't even tried to see Carmen.

I had about an hour at noon to think and became increasingly disgusted with what was taking place. I could be forced to leave the country because of the young squirt interrogating me. An investigation was being conducted and my future depended on his presentation of the evidence. I resented him and his power over me.

I dreaded seeing my interrogator enter the door again. This time he was in a hurry to get the forms filled out. "What political activities have you participated in? Do you have any communist friends?" Then another repeat of the series on where I went to high school, what I did after college, how I entered the country. I wondered if he was so disorganized that he had to keep repeating or if he was trying to wear me out. I decided he was probably just disorganized.

At 3:00 p.m. a colonel, the second-in-command of the Treasury police, arrived dressed in blue jeans and tennis shoes. He made it clear he was on his way to the beach but had been called in to get this case settled. He said he wanted to talk "Christian to Christian." He introduced himself as a member of a local Baptist church, a personal friend of Pat Robertson, and a supporter of the 700 Club and Youth With a Mission.

"You may find this experience difficult to understand right now," he said. "But all things work together for good for those that love the Lord. My mother used to tell me that when I was young and I still believe it."

He quoted Paul's instructions in Ephesians 6. "Slaves should obey their earthly masters and masters should treat their slaves with respect."

"That's proof that the class system is biblical," he continued. "God made some poor and others rich. The poor need to stay in their position and the rich need to be kind to them. Society couldn't function if it were any other way.

"You have to be careful reading the Bible with the poor. For example, if you just read the verse 'It's harder for a rich man to enter the kingdom of heaven than for a camel to pass through the eye of a needle,' they get the wrong idea. They think rich people can't be Christians. You have to give a balanced view."

I wondered if I would have been arrested if I had expressed God's love to the poor by handing out tracts in the street instead of trying to help them improve their inhumane living conditions. But I kept my questions to myself. All thoughts of being prophetic were suppressed by my desire to be released.

Finally he said he just had two questions. "Have you given political talks? Are you working with the guerrillas?" Satisfied with my responses, he said we would be released soon.

The interrogator finished his questions in about a half hour. I was elated at the sudden turn of events! They took me to an office where Blake was already waiting. Carmen arrived a few minutes later. She and Blake had been questioned but not intensely interrogated. The vice-consul and one of the MCCers who had come to deliver our bags with a change of clothes took us home instead!

We were released at 4:00 p.m. on Saturday afternoon, just as my father and stepmother arrived in the country for a long-planned vacation. Although they knew we had been arrested they had decided to come anyhow. Maureen picked them up at the airport not knowing we were being released. We had a joyful reunion that night!

Monday morning Carmen went back to Gotera with a friend. The six of us on the MCC team gathered to take stock of our feelings. Fear. Anger. Loss of control. Vulnerability. We were taken aback by the intensity of emotions expressed as we began to taste a bit of what Salvadorans faced day in and day out. How did they cope?

Each person shared. For the first time we were dealing with our raw emotions together. We had learned to cope superficially. But underneath the emotions were twisting and seething until they finally came bursting forth. Ron was practically burned-out after three intense years in El Salvador, and the decision-making responsibility for getting us released had fallen primarily on his shoulders.

No one knew how hard to push and someone had to decide. These were the in-between years in El Salvador's civil war after the atrocities of 1980 and 1981 and before minor harassment of foreigners had become commonplace. We didn't have contingency plans like we developed later. His emotional reserves already depleted, Ron laid his head down and sobbed.

We were frightened by the fact that we had suppressed such strong emotions for so long. Had we become mechanical? Were we in danger of becoming robots like the soldiers, capable of inhuman acts because we no longer thought or felt? It was sobering to realize our mental health was at stake. The incentive for being a genuine support system to each other never felt greater. In the years that followed, sometimes we succeeded and sometimes we failed.

I was humbled that day as I realized I was incapable of making it alone. I was also humbled and embarrassed at the way our Salvadoran friends mobilized around us. We had tasted so little of their reality and look what it had done to us. Would our commitment ever begin to compare with theirs? My respect for them grew even more as they listened to our fears of minor threats without reminding us of their own experiences of torture and exile. Will I ever be that gracious? Will my pain serve to make me more compassionate?

Early Tuesday morning I woke with a start. I had a clear image in my mind of riding my ten-speed bike over rolling hills, something I did often. I was competing with myself, trying to muscle my way to the top of the hill in the highest gear possible. By concentrating on the top, I could make it to the end. Legs pumping and chest heaving, I kept pushing because I knew I could soon coast down.

The image lasted no more than an instant but the message has had a major impact. I was treating the challenges of life like short hills I could muscle my way up in high gear—assuming I would then coast down.

But God was saying that life isn't that way. Life is like a long, gradual incline. There is no use pushing myself in high gear as if short-term goals are ends in themselves. So I may as well relax, gear down, and prepare for the long haul.

Picking up the pieces after our arrest wasn't easy. People in Cacaopera were shocked that Americans had been arrested. They saw us leave town with the soldiers. They heard the helicopter and even guessed that we left in it. But it never occurred to them that we weren't leaving of our own free will. They thought we were taking advantage of a quick ride. Knowing the army had arrested Americans made them fearful for their own safety. If they dared arrest Americans, what would they do to poor Salvadorans?

By the time I returned to Cacaopera the shock of the arrest had worn off a little. I was touched by the concern people demonstrated. They were afraid I wouldn't come back and were happy I was determined to continue. I did make changes, though. Realizing that my fears about security weren't just paranoia, I was able to admit my anxiety about going there alone. Maureen reworked her schedule so we could be together at least part of the time.

From that point on I felt more settled, confident I was where I was supposed to be. I found I was able to enter into people's lives in a way I hadn't before.

8

Caught Between Lies and Truth

As I entered more fully into people's lives, I became more sensitive to their fears. Trying to understand my own fear as well as the fear of others, I reflected on the relationship between fear and truth. Several incidents challenged me.

I walked to Tierra Blanca with Ricardo. "Don't worry," he told me. "We're safe because the army moved into the area last night."

I was startled. The presence of the army meant mortars, captures, checkpoints, and harassment. Was he serious about feeling safe?

As we walked, Ricardo told me he and his wife prayed every day that God wouldn't see fit to punish them any more. His twenty-one-year-old son moved into Cacaopera from their village because the army promised to protect the young people from the guerrillas. He had been there a short time when soldiers tortured and killed him. Ricardo's daughter witnessed the incident. "She died three months later from the shock of seeing him," he explained.

Approaching his house, he pointed out two places where bombs had recently fallen. He was glad they had missed the house. We talked about a neighbor hospitalized with shrapnel injuries from a mortar. Pausing for a minute at the sound of shelling in the distance, Ricardo searched the hills. Then he pointed out where the fighting was taking place. We saw smoke billowing from a fire set by the soldiers. They routinely burned large areas of the countryside so the guerrillas wouldn't be able to hide in the underbrush. The fires further damaged the already deforested hillsides and often destroyed crops.

I thought about Ricardo. Here was a man who prayed desperately, asking a loving God to stop punishing his family. The army, on the other hand, killed his son, almost bombed his house, and ruined the land which was his livelihood. Yet he said he felt safe with the army. His perspective seemed warped.

Was he afraid to admit he was fearful of the army? Maybe he didn't want to leave the impression he had done something wrong which would account for his fear of retaliation. But then I wondered if he could even admit to himself that he was scared. Blaming God for punishing him took his suffering out of the realm of human blame. There was nothing to be done except passively accept God's punishment.

Recognizing his fear of the army would be one step toward admitting his problems might have a human cause. That, in turn, could lead toward doing something about it, which was dangerous. The safest position for people controlled by fear is to try to appease those who hold the power of life and death over them.

I thought again about the woman who came to our door soon after we arrived. "The soldiers. No! I mean the guerrillas killed my husband," she said weeping. And about Concha, who told her story in a way that made it impossible to determine if she fled the army or the guerrillas. Living under the watchful eye of the army, they had no choice but to try not to antagonize.

I understood why they chose to appease the army but my heart ached. What does living a lie do to a person's dignity? What happens when we suppress what we know to be true even for understandable reasons?

There were other examples of people struggling with fear. I walked three hours up to a small village with Lucas. He explained that several weeks earlier he was walking the same path when he met a group of soldiers. One had a piece of flesh dangling from his bayonet. He bragged it was the tongue of a guerrilla.

Continuing, Lucas encountered the mutilated corpse of a young woman, a rebel combatant, probably about fifteen. He told me that as he knelt to pray the soldiers surrounded him, their guns cocked and aimed. They accused him of being a guerrilla sympathizer. He explained that it was his Christian duty to pray and then bury anyone he found, whether a guerrilla or a soldier.

When they continued to threaten him he quoted Matthew 10:28: "Do not be afraid of those who kill the body but cannot kill the soul." The soldiers left.

Lucas went to a nearby house for a shovel to dig the grave. Gradually the neighbors arrived, fearful the soldiers would return. They wondered if the humane act of burying a dead guerrilla was worth the risk.

"It's hard to be a faithful Christian," Lucas told me, shaking his head. He went on to say that he was no longer afraid. He was aware he would probably die for his faith but had chosen to follow the cross.

As I listened to other people recount the same incident, however, I realized that Lucas was struggling with fear more than he was willing to admit. He told his part the way he wished he would have played it. In reality, others had to encourage him to bury the body. He was the one wondering if it was worth the risk, anxious that the soldiers would return.

Knowing that about him didn't make me respect him less.

It helped me identify with him. He wasn't a saint who had achieved the impossible but someone, like me, struggling to be faithful despite fear.

Another incident demonstrated that truth is more than words. Working with Ana María every day kept me grounded in the realities of daily life for rural Salvadorans. She shared deeply of her experiences.

One morning Ana María was on her way to work when soldiers stopped her bus. There had been fighting the night before in the area she was coming from and the soldiers were more sinister than usual.

"Everyone off the bus," the officer ordered sharply. "Men on one side, women on the other."

They lined up single file.

A soldier started down the line of women. "What's your name? Where do you live? Where are you going?" His accusing tone made the most straightforward questions sound intimidating. The soldier came to the woman next to Ana María. "Your papers are expired," he said menacingly. "According to your documents you aren't from this area. What are you doing here?"

The woman tried to explain that her birth certificate was destroyed in a fire and she was trying to locate other papers. He threatened to arrest her and accused her of collaborating with the guerrillas. She wrung her hands nervously. Desperate. Trapped. Alone.

Then the soldier turned to Ana María. "Do you know this woman? Can you vouch for her?"

"Yes, I know her well," Ana María replied. "She's telling the truth." The soldier moved on.

Ana María had never met the woman. Did she lie? Technically she did. She said she knew someone she had never met before. But Ana María went beyond legalistic definitions of truth. She penetrated the barrier of divisions and brought a universal truth to light—the trembling woman beside her was her sister. There are no strangers in the kingdom of God.

Other lies were blatant, untrue no matter how defined. In November 1985 I was surprised to see a front page newspaper article declaring that twelve AID workers had been kidnapped by the guerrillas in Cacaopera. It supposedly happened while I was there. I could hardly believe something that major could take place without my hearing about it, so the next time I was in Cacaopera I asked. Nothing had happened. I was amazed by the thoroughness of the article. It even had quotes by the guerrilla kidnappers.

Lies against church workers felt more threatening. The colonel met with the leaders of the camps. He warned them to beware of Marxist priests and said that the war was started by catechists who held subversive meetings. He cautioned them to be on the lookout in the camps. His words frightened the catechists. One quit but the rest continued despite their fear.

While the catechists had nothing to do with Marxism or starting the war, they were "subversive" in the true meaning of the word. Ironically, it was a soldier who clearly pinpointed the threat church workers represented.

A literacy program had been started in Cacaopera. Several soldiers stood at the convent window one afternoon listening to the class. Afterward, the officer demanded to speak to the woman in charge.

"You're teaching these people how to think!" he accused.

He implied that it was all right to teach people to read—even the government supported literacy campaigns—but it wasn't acceptable to do it in a way that helped them learn to use their minds. People who think are more difficult to control with lies and propaganda.

Thinking about truth and lies clarified a point in relation to our arrest. I remembered one of the first questions asked. "Why are you working in Cacaopera when there are so many displaced in Gotera?" Our work in Cacaopera exposed the truth about the manipulation of humanitarian aid. I naively began working there because I saw the need. But in doing that I brought to light the fact that the army created the need which they met according to their own purposes. I interfered with their counterinsurgency plan.

I'm not sure exactly when I learned that the letter I read in Bolivia about El Salvador was a description of Cacaopera. I remember, though, that it was reassuring to realize the pull to Cacaopera began long before I knew anything about pacification programs or counterinsurgency warfare. I could trust that my motives were inspired by God, despite accusations to the contrary.

Bible passages about truth took on meaning in the midst of the lies and deceit around me. Jesus told Pilate that his reason for being in the world was to testify to the truth (John 18:37). Work in Cacaopera brought home the power and threat of standing for truth. In John 17:17, Jesus prayed that the disciples would be sanctified by the truth. A footnote in my Bible says that to be sanctified means "to make holy." I felt God challenging me to let truth move me toward holiness, to allow truth to change me. I remembered the words of a friend before I came to El Salvador. She asked if I had the courage not to face physical danger but to make personal changes.

During that first year and a half I felt stimuli to change bombarding me from all directions. Besides trying to figure out how to do health work in a politically volatile situation, I was also dealing with other issues. I was a Mennonite working with the Catholics, an American in El Salvador, and a pacifist in the middle of a war.

I wanted to be open to change but I felt lonely and vulnerable. The outward trappings of my identity were being stripped away; I was forced to define who I was from the inside out. I couldn't look to any one person or group to integrate the different aspects of myself.

I felt insecure as I recognized that there were shades of gray between my stark definitions of right and wrong. God was challenging me to enter deeply into the experiences of other people but doing that meant accepting that my well-defined boundaries weren't applicable to everyone. Entering this murky area was risky. I was afraid of being carried away by the stream. I realized, however, that staying safely on the riverbank would cut me off from the experiences I needed in order to grow.

Reading Scott Peck's book *A Road Less Traveled* was helpful. He says that for new growth to take place one has to get rid of the old. Loss of the old results in depression, which is a normal sign of change unless it becomes prolonged.

It was early 1985 when I struggled with the question of staying or leaving. I recognized that my vague sense of dissatisfaction wasn't necessarily an indication that I should leave. I decided to risk taking it, instead, as a sign that I was on the verge of change. I chose to stay; my heaviness lifted.

Thinking about the people who suppressed the truth because of fear made me sad. I understood why they avoided truth. Their physical survival depended on it. But they paid the emotional price of bondage to fear.

On the other side were people like Ana María who incarnated John 8:32: "You will know the truth, and the truth will set you free." Released from the control of fear, they risked their lives to put truth into practice. Then there were those like Lucas and me, vacillating between courage and fear in our struggle to be faithful.

9

"Primero Dios"

After two years in El Salvador, I returned to the U.S. for vacation. Feeling the need for solitude and quiet, I decided to spend a week of my vacation making a silent retreat.

I started my retreat by reading Psalm 139: "O Lord, you have searched me and you know me." Intimacy. To know and be known. The psalmist felt what I longed for. Struggling with loneliness, I wrote in my journal.

> Friends, heartfelt sharing, fighting, anger, respect, acceptance. I want to share my daily life with friends. I want a home, a place of security, a sanctuary in the midst of evil, stable relationships, community that is dependable enough to be worth the pain of building it.

The words came from deep within. Maureen and I had worked hard on our relationship. Our personalities and backgrounds were different, but we had become more than co-workers. We were friends. It was difficult to see her leave.

My internal struggle was already affecting my relationship with Marnetta, Maureen's replacement. Marnetta and I knew each other a little from college and came from similar backgrounds. I thought our relationship would be easy, that we could skip the hard part Maureen and I had worked through. In my need for intimacy, I tried to make her fill the gap Maureen was leaving. It was an unfair expectation.

I was also starting to feel overwhelmed by the work load. After almost two years of trying to figure out how to work, we had finally found some direction. I needed Marnetta to jump in and help out. But new workers need to define their own roles and Marnetta was no exception. My needs forced her into a role that wasn't hers. And her needs kept her from being able to talk to me about it. Our relationship was painful because of it.

"The pain of building community." I experienced it in the parish team, among the health workers, and with the MCC unit. Any illusions that the crisis of war would keep petty problems in perspective were shattered.

I had realized the year before that the stress made them worse. Now I was faced with the fact that three–year MCC commitments meant someone was coming or going every year. Just as we worked through our differences, the unit would change. I had to let go of my expectations that MCC volunteers would provide the stable community I felt I needed.

In the midst of my emotional turmoil, I reflected on occasions when I felt God's love. I was reassured by incidents that came to mind. Two friends in different countries dreamt about me the night Blake, Carmen, and I were arrested. One saw me surrounded by soldiers and the other pictured me being interrogated. They both felt led to pray for me.

A family friend, knowing we were in prison, went to bed with a heavy heart. He woke up in the middle of the night with the confidence that we were released. He was right.

There was no rational way my friends could have known what was happening. I was grateful to the Holy Spirit for speaking to them. I was grateful to my friends for listening and responding. Once more, I was humbled as I realized I was receiving God's love and grace.

I felt God's love through the poor I wanted to help. They accepted me in my impotence even when I couldn't accept myself. I didn't understand why I found myself getting angry at the people who came to our door in Gotera. Reflecting on a particular incident, I realized my anger was connected to feeling impotent.

It was Easter week and the pharmacy was closed. I tried to ignore the knock on our door but it persisted. Finally I answered it.

"The pharmacy is closed," I said curtly to the woman standing there. "You have to go to the hospital."

I wanted to slam the door but her eyes forced me to look at her face. I noticed for the first time that she was holding a sick child in her arms.

My tone softened. "Listen, I know the hospital is closed for Easter week but you have to demand your right for treatment. They can't just close the hospital for a whole week! At least the emergency room is open. Why don't you go there and insist on seeing a doctor?"

The frustrated woman poured out her story. Her husband had been killed the year before. She had left her other four children with a neighbor, had walked five hours, and ridden in a truck two more. Then she had to spend the night on a bench in the emergency room cradling her sick child in her arms. I berated myself for responding so sharply when I answered the door.

Why did I get angry at the people who came to us looking for help? They were desperate. I realized I lashed out at them because they reminded me of my impotence. What could I do to help the woman with her child? To really help? Giving her medicine was like putting a bandage strip on an ulcer. What about the next time? What about the thousands of people like her falling through the cracks of a dysfunctional health care system? We could never take care of everyone. The system had to change. But how?

My inability to face my own powerlessness was interfering with relationships. Displacing my anger and frustration, I did violence to people I cared about. I either had to face my impotence or leave.

When I was able to admit that I didn't have the answers, I felt God's love and acceptance through those I had been lashing out against. I apologized to the promoters in Cacaopera because other commitments kept me from spending more time with them. They were ready to move forward but couldn't because I didn't have time for the necessary training.

"Don't feel bad," one said reassuringly. "We know good things take time."

Blanca spoke similar words. Her son was sick and I was frustrated because I couldn't give the kind of help he needed. I wanted her to understand that I cared but didn't know what to do.

After I poured out my frustration, she said in all sincerity, "That's okay. I'm just glad you come to visit." How close I came to not doing even that much just because being with her made me face my impotence.

Forced military recruitment was another issue that bothered me. I had mixed feelings relating to the soldiers. On the one hand, they were mostly poor peasants forced into the army against their will. But even dressed in civilian clothes, they carried an air of belligerent authority that made them easy to pick out. Civilians were frequently injured by soldiers on leave carrying pistols and grenades.

Many of the army recruits came from the camps of displaced people. One day, the son of a good friend was taken as soldiers swept through the camp.

"It's so hard to see my son with the same army that massacred my family," Lupe told me. "It would be bad enough to lose him for a worthy cause, but to think he might die for nothing is almost more than I can bear. We're Christians. I tried to convince him to go to seminary so he wouldn't be recruited, but he doesn't like to study. He promised when he left that he wouldn't kill anyone in cold blood. What can I do?"

Recruiting was usually done at the end of the month. No matter what their political beliefs, people were united in trying to prevent young men from being conscripted. A ten-year-old girl was riding home in the back of a pickup when she overheard two soldiers in civilian clothes discussing their plan to recruit the teenagers playing soccer.

The girl jumped off the truck at the edge of town and hurried to the soccer field. "They're coming to recruit," she said breathlessly.

The soccer players immediately dispersed. They were welcomed into nearby houses where they hid in closets and under beds. By the time the soldiers arrived, there wasn't a young man in sight.

"It isn't only that I'm afraid my son will be killed," an anxious mother told me. "It's the way they change once they're in the army. My son is a good boy. He respects me and works hard. In the army they learn to smoke and drink. The power goes to their heads and they don't respect anyone anymore."

What turns decent peasant boys into killers capable of massacring women and children? I thought about the mural of the skull and cross bones painted on the barracks wall. I shuddered when I saw it. Soldiers often left graffiti on the walls of places they stayed during army maneuvers. An abandoned church had a graphic drawing with the words, "We rape the pueblo."

I saw a soldier with a T-shirt which said, "Kill them all. Let God judge." MCC volunteers in a small town found their streets littered with army propaganda declaring, "We are the fiancés of death." I heard stories about initiation rites which included animal sacrifices and drinking blood. Only demonic forces could exalt the worship of death. Few young men were strong enough to resist evil's seductive influence.

I occasionally glimpsed the psychological pressure the conscripts experienced. We always knew when there was a batch of new recruits. They would march awkwardly through the streets with their heads shaved, dressed in poorly fitting uniforms and oversized boots. Many didn't know left from right. The officers would yell and curse, trying to teach them to march in step and do exercises they had never done before.

A group of about fifteen stopped outside our window. A lieutenant was teaching them to do push-ups but several just couldn't get the hang of it. The officer rewarded those who learned quickly with the privilege of punishing the slower ones. Each time someone did it wrong he found himself kicked or hit by one of his buddies.

I cringed as I watched them beat each other. The officer egged on the strong ones, encouraging them to beat the others harder and harder. Wanting to please the lieutenant, they complied until they learned the thrill of power for its own sake.

The most blatant example of psychological pressure came unexpectedly in May, as I waited for the promoters who were going to participate in our first week-long health course. I was nervous. All the planning had been done through notes and messages, since the participants lived in conflictive areas where we couldn't visit. The idea was to meet in Gotera and travel together to San Salvador for the course. Did the messages get through correctly? Would they really be willing to risk attending a health course?

Finally I heard a knock, the first arrival. She assured me more were on their way. I was relieved. Then another woman came.

She could hardly wait for the customary introductions before she broke the news. "Chente, the other promoter from my community, was recruited as we entered Gotera."

We consulted quickly among each other. The consensus was that we must try to get him out before they took him to the barracks. We hurried to the priest's house, hoping one of them could go with us or at least let us use the car.

Padre Martín was studying in his room. Before I had even finished explaining, he grabbed the car keys, ready to go. I was relieved, since priests have influence in Latin American society.

My heart sank as we approached the area where the promoter had been recruited. I didn't see anyone. Then Carmen spotted them. About twenty young men were lined up in two rows. We quickly picked out Chente from the description the woman had given us.

Martín talked to the officer, explaining that Chente worked with the church.

"We all have an obligation to work for peace," the officer responded. "You do it by being a priest and I do it by being a soldier. Chente can work for peace just as well through the army as through the church."

The soldier turned to the teenagers lined up in front of him and exclaimed, "You want to be in the army, don't you!" It was more a command than a question. "You want me to be your officer."

He looked at a new recruit. "What do you think? Should I let Chente go?" The young man fidgeted, not sure how to respond.

"No, he should stay," the recruit finally said nervously.

"See there," the officer said, smiling at Martín. "I can't let him go unless everyone is in agreement." He asked four or five more what they thought.

By that time the answer the officer wanted was clear and each negative response was more emphatic. Then he asked the whole group.

"No!" they shouted in unison.

The officer called Chente forward. I prayed desperately. With the group pressure so strong, I wouldn't have been surprised to hear Chente say he wanted to stay. But instead of asking, the officer unexpectedly changed his mind and said he could go.

I was relieved but shaken by the power of the psychological pressure I had just observed. Trapped by fear, the young men wanted to please the one in power. They were easy targets for the officer's manipulative techniques.

Chente was released, and the course went on as planned. I was enthusiastic about training health promoters from the isolated, conflictive zones. We had finally found a positive way to work with the people most cut off from medical services.

Spending time with them gave me insights into life in guerrilla-controlled areas. I was surprised to learn that over 5,000 civilians lived north of the Torola River, the unofficial boundary between government and guerrilla territory.

The difference between my friends in the displaced camps and the promoters from the conflictive zones impressed me. Those who had chosen to stay in the conflictive areas had dealt with fear and death. They carried a sense of quiet dignity which contrasted sharply with the self-deprecating humbleness of the displaced. Rosa explained their freedom.

> Several years ago whenever we were bombed we had to decide whether we were going to stay or leave. It kept us in constant emotional turmoil. But even though we know we might die in our homes, we are much happier now that the decision is made. We have our fiestas again. And when the bombing starts we keep on going. We all have to die sometime and we're not going to ruin our lives wondering when it will happen.

The life-filled health promoters helped me in a way I

hadn't anticipated. Their playfulness was contagious; I found myself becoming less reserved as I entered into the fun. I benefited as much as they from the participatory learning techniques we tried to implement. We played games designed to encourage the timid ones and put on hilarious skits to help them become more comfortable in front of groups.

I reveled in watching the promoters express themselves by drawing symptoms of different diseases and making collages of the kingdom of God. They had never had the opportunity to draw and color, to cut and paste.

I loved the promoters' enthusiasm as they gained confidence. My words of encouragement could have been directed at myself. "It doesn't have to be perfect. Relax. Give it a try. No one else cares if it isn't just right." Perhaps I was concerned about the participation of the timid ones because I also struggle with timidness. In freeing them, I was freeing myself.

We started every morning with a biblical reflection. One morning we read Matthew 8:18-22, where Jesus demands that the disciples leave everything to follow him. "Follow me, and let the dead bury their own dead," he tells them.

One participant commented, "We want to follow but we don't want to leave anyone behind. We end up trying to carry the dead with us, but that only bogs us down. We have to move on and leave behind the ones who choose not to come along."

I was challenged not only by her words but also by her example. What excess baggage was holding me back? I remembered my retreat and God's call to let go. Letting go was clearly a continuous process, not something I could do once and for all.

The collages the promoters made picturing the kingdom of God also provided food for thought in their description of the kingdom of God as justice, peace, love, food, medicines, equality. "The kingdom of God is among us but still coming closer," one promoter said.

We also discussed the values of the kingdom of the world. "Instead of concentrating on tearing down the kingdom of the world, we need to emphasize building up the kingdom of God," Juan José admonished us.

I appreciated their grasp of the transcendence of the kingdom. They understood it as a concrete reality that had arrived—but not yet in fullness. Juan José's comment about building up rather than tearing down reminded me of John Howard Yoder's thoughts in *The Politics of Jesus* concerning the role of the church. "The very existence of the church . . . is itself a proclamation, a sign, a token to the Powers that their unbroken dominion has come to an end."[6]

Yoder suggests that the church isn't called to take the offensive against the powers or "tear down the kingdom of the world," in Juan José's words. Simply by being Christian community, the church unmasks the illusion that the powers of the world are in control.

Perhaps the discussion that had the greatest impact on me that year was one about mental health. Most promoters had never even heard the term "mental health." But life experience had given them profound insights. "When we don't say what we think and feel, we become sick," one person explained.

Another expressed his understanding of poor mental health and self-centeredness. "When we're in poor mental health we stop thinking about other people. We become self-centered. And the more self-centered we become the worse our mental health becomes."

We divided into small groups, in which the health promoters listed the obstacles they faced in their work. Some obstacles were logistical. "When it rains we can't cross the river because we don't have a bridge." "It's a two-day walk to town." "I have to help my father in the fields."

But most obstacles had to do with the army. "We're harassed at checkpoints." "Soldiers don't even let us take enough food to our homes, much less medicines." "We don't have the freedom to speak the truth about injustice." "The soldiers capture us and threaten to bomb our homes."

The promoters spoke in generalities about army abuses but I knew of several recent incidents that confirmed what they said. Residents of four villages were summoned to a military command post where they were told their homes would be bombed if they didn't leave. A young man immediately began circulating a petition asking the Red Cross to help them stay. The next day he was found dead in a ditch, his ears and fingers cut off.

Checkpoints were strict in some areas. After walking two hours to buy food, villagers weren't allowed to take home more than a three-day supply of corn. One woman was turned back at a checkpoint for not having military permission for her purchases. She was carrying an onion, a pound of salt, and a bar of soap.

I felt overwhelmed as each group shared its list of obstacles. Were we crazy to try to do health work in conflictive zones? What about the risks the promoters were taking? Was I responsible for their involvement in work that could mean being captured or killed?

After they presented the obstacles, we discussed how much impact they thought they could have on their communities by working as health promoters. I was taken aback by their responses. They were humble about their limited abilities but clear that it was worthwhile to try. The stress they lived with had not conquered their spirits.

Straying from the lesson plan, I asked the question uppermost on my mind. "Aren't you afraid?"

"Of course we're afraid," Hilario said smiling. "We'd be crazy not to be. But we're also committed. It's our commitment, not our fear, that determines what we do."

I had thought about the relationship between fear and truth. Now the promoters articulated the relationship between fear and commitment. Commitment breaks the bondage of fear. My concern that I was somehow responsible if something happened to them was irrelevant. Their commitment and understanding of the consequences far surpassed mine.

Two years later, Hilario was murdered taking medicines to his village. He was last seen being beaten by soldiers and loaded onto a helicopter. All efforts to locate him were futile. Several weeks later, the decomposing pieces of Hilario's mutilated body were found in a woods.

Another health promoter, Alonzo, taught me the meaning of the common Salvadoran expression "Primero Dios" or "God willing." It was the week before the first course and Alonzo was in Gotera. I was tense and wanted to know who was going to attend.

"Are you coming to the course?" I asked.

"Primero Dios," he responded.

His answer wasn't definite enough to suit me. I asked another way. Again, his only response was "Primero Dios."

"Listen, I need to know how many to plan for. It's only a week away. Can't you say for sure if you're going to come or not?"

Then it was his turn to be forthright. "I hope to come," he said. "But lots of things could interfere with my plans. I might get sick. Something could happen to one of my children. I could be captured. There could be shooting or bombing so I couldn't travel. Anything is possible. I can only say 'Primero Dios' I will make it to the course."

I was humbled by his awareness that our lives are determined by factors beyond our control. I had had many opportunities to experience the truth of his words—mother's illness, transportation problems in Bolivia, the war. It was a hard lesson for me to accept even though I was reminded of it over and over again.

The last of the three week-long courses was scheduled for the end of October. But once more I was reminded I wasn't in control. On October 10, 1986, an earthquake hit San Salvador. It killed over 1,000 people, injured 10,000, and left 200,000 homeless. I was in Cacaopera when it happened and didn't even feel the tremor.

When rumors of an earthquake started circulating, my new co-worker Patty and I turned on the radio. The reports were sketchy and emphasized that everything was under control. It was impossible to tell how serious the earthquake was. The sunset that evening was particularly striking. Vibrant pinks and reds bathed the town in color. A disaster in the capital seemed a faraway nightmare. I went to bed that night wanting to believe the damage had been slight.

The earthquake was the only subject of conversation the next morning in Cacaopera. Rumors spread like wildfire. It seemed people were assuming that anyone they knew in San Salvador had been killed. I disliked the climate of fear.

Patty and I went on with scheduled plans that day but decided to go into San Salvador the next. As we approached the capital I craned my neck out the window looking for signs of the earthquake. I saw nothing unusual and began to feel foolish. Maybe I too had gotten carried away by the rumors.

Arriving at the outskirts, we changed to a local city bus. The closer we got to the MCC house, the more signs of destruction I saw. We heard that our neighborhood had been hit hard.

My feelings flipped to the opposite extreme. In my desire not to let myself be influenced by unconfirmed reports, I began to think perhaps I had denied the reality that people I knew could have been killed or injured.

The bus veered around landslides and uprooted trees. Finally the driver said he couldn't go any further. As we continued on foot I saw crumbled walls and caved-in roofs.

Rubble was everywhere. Makeshift plastic shelters covered beds, tables, and personal belongings. By the time we got to the MCC house my heart was thumping.

I was relieved that the building was still standing. Passing through the Lutheran offices in front, I saw that the walls were badly damaged. Anxiously I entered our house and walked from room to room. The bookshelves had fallen, scattering books all over the library floor. The big planters in the patio had broken. But there was no serious damage. The newer cement walls held better than the old adobe ones in the front office.

Foreign aid flows in after a natural disaster. I watched the boxes of medicine being loaded onto trucks. Aspirin, Tylenol, antibiotics—the same medicines we desperately needed in the rural areas. I rejoiced at the display of international support for those suffering from the earthquake, but my heart ached for the thousands who had been isolated and forgotten during the war. They also needed food and medicine. Who cared about them?

Meanwhile the war continued. The FMLN declared a unilateral truce October 11, but the army rejected it the following day. Armed men watched the Lutheran church as relief workers came and went. Four people were captured the day after the earthquake. Bombing continued around the Guazapa volcano. The government denied landing rights to fifteen planeloads of relief aid because it was destined for the church instead of the government. The war took priority, even during a national disaster.

10

God Is Everywhere

Although I was feeling fulfilled in my work, I had a dream that seemed to say I needed to process what was happening inside. I dreamed I was looking for a Bible passage but the books were out of order. I felt frustrated and confused. The dream left me with questions. My work was going well. What was out of order inside? Why the confusion?

The pace of life in 1986 and 1987 was hectic. The programs we had started functioned well as long as we dedicated enough energy to overcome the obstacles. I willingly poured out all the energy I could muster, but I began to wonder if I was burning out. I longed for my vacation in March. I counted the days until I could have a day off, sometimes several weeks away. With overnight trips to the scattered villages and living in both Gotera and Cacaopera, I rejoiced when I slept in the same bed several nights in a row.

I began to wonder if it was time to leave El Salvador. A year of seminary was an attractive option, as was nurse practitioner training. I applied to schools and made plans to return to the U.S. in January 1988. Since I had plenty of vacation time left, I decided I would go to Guatemala for a week every two or three months. I found a convent that rented rooms and realized with the first trip that days of solitude were exactly what I needed. My spirit revived as I listened to God and to the voices clamoring within me.

I read *New Seeds of Contemplation* by Thomas Merton and jotted numerous quotes in my journal. As I tentatively followed God's invitation to "risk jumping into the stream," I began to realize God was bigger than my narrow definitions. I experienced the truth that Merton expressed. "God is everywhere. [Divine] truth and love pervade all things as the light and heat of the sun pervade our atmosphere."[7] Merton also articulated the creative vibrancy of faith I was beginning to taste: "Every moment and every event of [human] life on earth plants something in [one's] soul."[8]

In June I went to Guatemala, where I wrote in my journal about my faith in relation to the world around me.

> Somewhere I picked up the subtle sense that everything around me was out to destroy my faith; that faith was so delicate that we had to isolate it and protect it from the worldly influences that would ruin it if we gave them half a chance. Now I'm seeing that God is present in every aspect of life. What God created can't destroy true faith. It can only knock holes in our false images of piety.

I realized I was expecting rules to protect my faith. My need for defined boundaries went way back. My mother said I came home from first grade one day and declared I was the only Christian in my whole class.

"How do you know?" she asked.

"Because I'm the only one who doesn't say 'ain't,' " I stated proudly.

God was calling me to let go of the security of legalism and enter into life led by the Spirit. Relationships with people around me were affected by my growing awareness of God's all-encompassing presence and increased willingness to step toward the unknown. I was less legalistic and therefore more open to looking past outward appearances. This brought me into contact with some interesting people.

I was more aware of God's presence with the poor. I became interested in intentional communities as an option after I returned to the U.S. And I painfully realized the truth of Thomas Merton's words, "As long as we are on the earth, the love that unites us will bring us suffering from our very contact with one another, because this love is the resetting of a Body of broken bones."[9] I was forced to look at my own personal relationships and wondered if I was involved in the healing or breaking of bones.

Looking for a different house in Cacaopera reminded me lifestyle issues must be decided in the context of personal relationships, not theoretical guidelines. We were offered a new house at the edge of the camp where I was working. Living there would have meant much informal interaction with people I wanted to relate to, but the contrast of a nice house beside the squalid camp was too much for me.

I had to admit, though, that I wouldn't have been as uncomfortable with the same house in another location. I realized that living in close contact with the poor forced me to examine my own life, and that I needed them to help me keep lifestyle issues alive.

During my vacation in the U.S., I struggled with feeling vaguely depressed. It wasn't the "high" that my last trip had been. Several factors were involved. After a year of hectic activity, I could finally let my defenses down. Suppressed emotions of fear, loneliness, and feeling overwhelmed had space to surface. But—though it was clear many in my family and church cared—few understood.

I felt isolated. I had changed and home could never be the same again. I grieved my loss. My feelings were also affected by thinking that in a year I would be returning to the U.S. to live. During my vacation I tried to see myself living in the U.S. again and realized the adjustment would be difficult.

I was struck by the number of hurting people in middle-class churches. People struggled to find healing from sexual abuse, child abuse, alcohol abuse, drug abuse. Why all the abuse? Why were people whom society had defined as "successful" struggling with so much inner pain?

Reflecting on self-identity, Thomas Merton said,

> People who know nothing of God and whose lives are centered on themselves, imagine that they can only find themselves by asserting their own desires and ambitions and appetites in a struggle with the rest of the world. They try to become real by appropriating for themselves some share of the limited supply of created goods and then emphasizing the difference between themselves and others who have less than they, or nothing at all.[10]

Merton's thoughts made me think that North Americans trampling over others to get to the top wasn't due simply to society's valuing of getting ahead. The problem seemed deeper, involving how we see ourselves in relation to others.

In the vocabulary I had become used to in El Salvador, we are a society of oppressed and oppressors. We dominate those with less and are dominated by those with more as we compete to assert our own identity. We suffer from being abused and abusing others.

It was easy to be judgmental of those I identified as oppressors, but I became more compassionate when I realized that I, too, was an oppressor on a personal level. My relationship with my roommate, Patty, had its ups and downs. I learned a great deal from her about popular education and appreciated the music she brought into my life. But a minor incident made us realize that oppressor/oppressed dynamics between us kept our relationship from flourishing.

We had gone to Guatemala to introduce our two Salvadoran co-workers to health programs there. On the way back to our hotel after a long day, we got off the bus about five or six blocks from our lodging.

"Is there a bus from here to the hotel?" Patty asked.

"I'm not sure. Probably," I said as I started walking.

Feeling tension that evening, we discussed what was wrong. Several issues emerged, including my being insensitive and dominating on our way back to the hotel. I was puzzled. I wasn't sure what I had done. As we talked, it became clear that Patty hadn't only been asking if there were buses. She was really saying that she was tired and wanted a ride. She resented me for walking on without taking her into account.

I had heard only the superficial question. If I had understood that she wanted to ride the bus, I would have been willing to comply. We realized there were many similar examples in our relationship.

Oppressed people are typically "voiceless." They have never learned to speak up for themselves. When they start they often do it awkwardly, like a bird learning to fly. Oppressors, on the other hand, are typically deaf. They shut their ears to the voices struggling to make themselves heard. Their deafness isn't necessarily conscious. In our relationship, Patty was like the oppressed needing to speak clearly, and I was like the oppressor needing to listen.

I wasn't dominating Patty intentionally but that didn't lessen the effects on her. I had to accept my share of the responsibility, even though Patty, by not clearly expressing her needs, sometimes allowed herself to be dominated. The lack of communication damaged our relationship, and our wounded relationship hurt us both.

I tried to apply what I was learning personally on a broader level. Does God ask more than good intentions? A short parable in Anthony de Mello's *Song of the Bird* caught my attention.

"What on earth are you doing?" said I to the monkey when I
saw him lift a fish from the water and place it on a tree.
"I'm saving it from drowning," was the reply.[11]

It was easy to see the monkey's behavior was inappropri-
ate. The monkey, knowing he would drown if he were in the
water, did what he thought helpful. He didn't understand
that fish are different from monkeys. His intentions were
good—but that didn't help the poor fish dying in the tree.

When we don't understand the perspective of others we
respond inappropriately. Sixty-three percent of Salvadorans
have no access to medical care. There is a waiting list of
20,000 people for elective surgery at the public hospital.
Seventy-five percent of the children under five are malnourished. There is 50 percent unemployment.[12] But not understanding the plight of the poor, the U.S. government began
sending military aid.

Thus good, well-meaning North American Christians
contribute to the deaths of poor Salvadorans. Doing it unin-
tentionally didn't mean fewer Salvadorans died because of
U.S. foreign policy support of their repressive government.

Nor did our lack of awareness mean we, too, weren't neg-
atively affected. We paid a high price, for our own healing
depends on sharing food with the hungry and providing
shelter for the homeless (Isa. 58:7-8). We abuse ourselves
and others when we "shut our ears to the cry of the poor"
(Prov. 21:13) and don't recognize that to know God is to de-
fend "the cause of the poor and needy" (Jer. 22:16). We are
healed as we discover that our own true identity is based not
on competition, but on responding compassionately to the
weak and needy.

Daily life kept my theological musings grounded in reality. It was tempting to want escape. Theoretically loving my
sister or brother across the world was easier than loving
people so close to me they chipped away at my rough edges.

I felt consoled by Merton's words about the love uniting us bringing suffering because it's a love that resets a body of broken bones. At least the pain of building community was part of the healing process.

My main project in Cacaopera during 1987 was a nutrition study comparing the nutritional status of the children in the camp with those in an outlying village. As in the past, searching for root causes of malnutrition brought me face to face with politics.

I initially planned to do only a straight comparison of nutritional status. In talking to the families in the camp, however, I realized many of their children had died. I began asking why. According to their responses, 16 percent of the children under fifteen had died of measles and 25 percent under five had been or were being treated for tuberculosis.

I was appalled but not surprised, given the cycle of disease and malnutrition. Malnourished children are more susceptible to disease, and being sick makes them more malnourished. When I first weighed all the children under five in 1985, none had a normal weight for their age.

The nutrition program temporarily helped the worst cases but I wanted a longer term approach. Realizing the families couldn't afford to buy high-protein foods like milk and eggs, I included questions about economics in the nutrition study. Most of the families earned their living making jute hammocks and bags. Calculating prices, I found they cleared the equivalent of about $1.50 per person per week, way under the minimum wage of $2.00 per day.

I was angry when I learned that the people who bought the hammocks took them to the city and sold them at double the price. Why couldn't the displaced form a cooperative and sell the hammocks themselves?

I'll never forget Jorge's response to my idea. "We are poor because we're like disobedient children who deserve God's punishment." He ended the conversation, unwilling to listen to an idea that might imply he was resisting God's will.

If we couldn't do much to improve their diet, maybe we could break the cycle of malnutrition by lowering the transmission of communicable diseases. The year before, two toilets had been built and a water line brought to the camp. But the town had an inadequate water supply since the mayor had used water project money to buy himself a truck.

The water was distributed to different neighborhoods several hours a day, and people in the camp were lucky if there was even enough to fill their jugs, much less to flush the toilets. We discussed what they might be able to do to receive more water. The discussion was interesting, but the people took no concrete action. After all, if poverty was God's punishment, then resisting it might make their situation even worse.

I began to wonder if there might be interest in moving out of the camp. The families had originally come from the countryside. Maybe they would be willing to move back. It seemed the only way to do more than stopgap nutrition programs. I became cautiously optimistic when several families expressed interest.

We had several meetings where we discussed giving those who moved out tin to rebuild their homes and fertilizer to plant their first crop. We were still in the discussion stage when another project "neutralized" us. A Christian relief organization targeted Cacaopera as a priority. They built new tin shacks, gave each family some jute to make hammocks, and donated food for six months. Their palliative measures appeased people long enough to squelch the impetus behind what we were planning. No one left the camp, and San José became a permanent slum.

Did the organization realize what it was doing? Were they consciously part of the government supported pacification programs that kept the poor placated in their squalor? I will never know, but their timing was perfect to squelch the tiny seeds of initiative that were just starting to take root. Giving their intentions the benefit of the doubt didn't change the effects on the people in San José. I felt sad and defeated.

I was reminded again that I wasn't in control when rumors that the guerrillas were going to attack the military headquarters in Gotera circulated. I hoped we wouldn't be home when it happened, since our house was located in the middle of the military zone.

I had no reason to suspect anything when I went to bed the night of May 1. I was sound asleep when something awakened me. Disoriented, I jumped out of bed and grabbed my house dress, a souvenir *mumu* sent as a gift from Hawaii. I thought I was in a hotel in Guatemala.

Hearing footsteps coming toward my room, I was sure I was about to be robbed. I quickly slammed the door shut, my heart pounding. I was still standing there, mumu in hand, when I heard someone calling my name. I thought it was the friend I had recently visited in Guatemala, so I opened the door.

"Patty! Where did you come from?" I exclaimed as my housemate pushed her way into my room.

She stared at me blankly, trying to figure out if I was still half-asleep or already in shell shock. "The guerrillas are attacking the barracks," she said.

"They can't be," I mumbled. "See, the fan is still going. The first thing the guerrillas would do is cut the electricity." Just then the fan slowly purred to a halt.

We sat listening for a moment as the scattered explosions increased to a cacophony of mortars, grenades, M-60's, and M-16's. I was mesmerized by the flashes of exploding light. Patty and I calmly discussed how far away the mortars were landing. Then several fell so close we could hear plaster filtering down. The soldier stationed by our house fired. The crack of his rapid-fire gun made my ears ring and heart race.

What do you do while waiting for a poorly aimed mortar

to explode on top of you? Patty and I sang. We sang hymns and choruses. We sang in Spanish and English. Any song we could think of, we sang. Although my insides were quivering, I experienced God's peace in a way that is impossible when I can delude myself that I'm in control.

My active thoughts turned to nonviolence. Each gut-wrenching jolt of a bomb falling nearby brought home the destructive power of firearms. The consequences of the peace position I had always taken for granted were becoming clear. Did I have the courage to choose nonviolence?

After an hour and a half, the shooting gradually subsided. I burst out laughing as I thought about how I woke thinking I was being robbed in Guatemala. Our pent-up emotions found welcome relief as Patty and I laughed hilariously.

Wondering if the house had been hit, I walked to the store room closest to the barracks wall. I was relieved to find it intact. Several fluorescent light bulbs were shattered on the floor and the 100 pound bags of powdered milk were in disarray, proof that it wasn't just our imagination that the house had been shaking.

My respect for the people who chose to stay in their homes despite the bombing grew as I tasted some of their fear and helplessness. Knowing I was scared even with the protection of brick walls, my heart went out to the displaced, huddled behind walls made of nothing but cornstalks.

The war was becoming commonplace, and I took it all in stride. I wondered what was happening to me, though. I hardly responded emotionally any more unless the case was particularly blatant or I knew the people involved. Was I becoming hardened? Or did I have to shut off my emotions to cope with the pressure? I had little time to ponder those questions. In October 1987 a group of Salvadoran refugees from Mesa Grande, Honduras, returned to resettle in their homes and I left Gotera to accompany them.

11

Hating All Violence

The refugees living in Mesa Grande since the early '80s had been talking for months about returning to their homes in El Salvador. Of approximately 10,000 refugees, 4,000 returned in October 1987 and other groups followed. They were concerned that, after eight years in the camp, their children were growing up without learning to work in the fields. There had also been human rights violations by the Honduran army. The refugees felt as if they were prisoners in the camp, unable to leave even to buy food. "We all have to die sometime and we want to die in our homes," one woman explained.

The returning refugees were divided into five groups, each going to a different location. I joined the group headed for Las Vueltas, since it was located in the parish where Maureen had worked her last year and we knew the two priests. When the buses loaded with refugees finally crossed the border Sunday afternoon, I climbed on one of them. People were elated. I enjoyed listening to their excited chatter as they pointed out plants and trees they had missed in Honduras.

But as it grew dark, the atmosphere became more subdued. Because of the repatriation, there were several army checkpoints set up. Seeing the soldiers brought back painful memories. Combined with the excitement of successfully crossing the border was the uncertainty of what lay ahead.

It was 11:00 Sunday evening before we arrived at the small town where we would spend the night. The last several hours were on a dirt road; traveling with a caravan of buses stirred up so much dust we had to close the windows. It was hot, and the stench of sweat and urine filled the bus. With all the stops, the four-hour trip took almost nine hours. I was glad to stretch out to sleep on the sidewalk, a luxury compared to the cramped, hot bus.

The terrain was now too rough for the buses to continue, so we waited two days for trucks that would take us within four kilometers of Las Vueltas. After that we went on foot, since only small jeeps could navigate the road.

I didn't foresee living in Las Vueltas long-term. But I decided to stay past my proposed January departure date until May, when an MCC couple might be able to continue health work in the parish. In Las Vueltas I fulfilled some of the dreams I had for Gotera.

I thrived on the simple lifestyle. Another foreign pastoral worker and I lived in one room with a dirt floor. We slept in hammocks, bathed in the river, and shared our lives with our neighbors. The interaction with people was a natural part of daily life. There were no nice houses and convent walls to become barriers.

The time was ripe for health work throughout the parish, so from the beginning my work went beyond the clinic in Las Vueltas. Maureen had planted the seeds in 1986, when she spent a year studying *Where There Is No Doctor* with small groups in some of the villages. Several people had then attended a health promoter course sponsored by the archdiocese. They were waiting for follow-up to get their small clinics started.

The health promoters were enthusiastic. I enjoyed walking from village to village visiting them. I covered eight villages along a thirteen-mile stretch of road. The army was rarely present, and I reveled in the freedom to walk when and where I wished.

Several months after I moved to Las Vueltas, I dreamed I went to the pool in the stream where I always bathed. The pool had dried up. I moved further upstream, where I found a door in a cement wall. Walking through, I saw a beautiful pool overflowing with water. I bathed there but felt awkward and vulnerable since it was a new spot.

The dream seemed to indicate I needed to move on. What was meaningful in the past had dried up; I was entering new pools. I felt uncomfortable as I got used to the changes, but I knew I couldn't turn back.

Returning to their homes brought back memories for the refugees, many traumatic and painful. Having learned not to ask the displaced in Gotera many questions, I was initially hesitant in Las Vueltas as well. I didn't want to dig into old wounds they weren't ready to open. But I soon learned they were eager to share their experiences. I was glad to listen, since it seemed important for them to talk and also helped me gain a better understanding of their past.

I was inspired by the signs of God people found in the midst of their trauma. Cruz told of fleeing the soldiers with 700 people, mostly women and children. It was the rainy season, and their wet feet were covered with sores—some infected and crawling with maggots. They were so desperate for food that they made tortillas from banana shoots and the heart of papaya trees.

"It was dangerous with so many small children," Cruz said. "Their crying could give away our hiding place. But God made the soldiers blind and deaf just like in the Bible.

"We were scared because the babies were crying and the soldiers were on a hill close-by. I expected them to come after us any minute but they didn't. Later the guerrillas captured one soldier and asked if he or his buddies had heard crying. He said that they had heard a noise but thought it was a swarm of wasps."

Cruz continued reminiscing. "Another time I was hiding with my husband and three children in a creek bed when we unexpectedly smelled cigarette smoke. Looking up, we saw soldiers passing beside us. We sat paralyzed, hardly daring to breathe. We didn't even have time to crouch down and hide. But they didn't see us. I'm so grateful to God for making them blind.

"Not everyone was so lucky, though," she said. "A young mother tried to keep her baby from crying while the soldiers passed. The lives of the whole group depended on it. In desperation she finally stuffed a rag in the baby's mouth and the baby suffocated. The poor mother was beside herself with guilt and loss, but we had to keep going. We didn't even have time to bury the baby, so the mother wrapped her in a cloth, folded her little arms across her chest, and laid her beside the path."

Margarita was my 70-year-old neighbor. I sometimes found myself rushing past her house hoping she wouldn't see me, since once she started talking it was hard to get away. But one afternoon she caught me. I was inspired and humbled by what she shared, especially because in my busyness I almost missed God speaking through her.

She said she wanted to tell me of a miracle God had worked in her life. One night as she fled soldiers, shrapnel injured her leg. She spent two weeks in a makeshift hospital. When she rejoined the group she was so weak she could hardly walk. She had trouble keeping up with the rest, and fell so far behind she got lost.

Margarita spent seventeen days wandering the mountains. Already weak from her injury, and without food, she soon found herself unable to continue searching for her friends. When two men finally found her she was so weak she couldn't even talk.

But the miracle she wanted to share wasn't being rescued. "The mountains are cold at night," she told me. "I just had the thin cotton dress I was wearing—but do you know what? Every night I laid down on the cold, hard ground and slept soundly. Isn't God good!"

I left her house shaking my head in wonderment at Margarita's faith. What would it take for me to develop eyes to see God's presence as Margarita did?

Several people in Las Vueltas had survived the Sumpul River massacre. Elena, a vivacious fifty-year-old woman, told me what happened.

> There were about a thousand of us, mostly women and children. We were cornered with the soldiers in front and the river behind us when the army started firing, driving us like cattle toward the river.
>
> My husband and I were part of the pushing, shoving crowd desperately making our way down the narrow path. Our only hope was to cross the river into Honduras.
>
> Then helicopters came and fired on us from above. My husband was hit in the face. His head was blown to bits, but I didn't even stop. People were falling all around me. I got to the river, but the Honduran soldiers were shooting at us from the other side. People tried to cross anyway but many couldn't swim. If they weren't shot, they drowned.
>
> Fortunately I could swim, so I went downstream and swam underwater. Every time I came up for air the soldiers fired on me, but I made it across. From my hiding place I saw a soldier throw a baby up in the air and catch it on his bayonet. The river was red with the blood of over 600 people killed that day.

I felt as if I were in seminary that year, a seminary of intense life experiences. My main subjects were suffering and violence. As people recounted their stories, I tried to understand their perspective on God and suffering.

Initially, I asked something like, "Did you ever get angry

at God for the suffering you've experienced?" Or, "If God is good, how could God let you suffer so much?"

But I soon realized such questions were foreign to them. They didn't understand what I was talking about. I started prefacing my questions, explaining, "When North American Christians suffer, we tend to think God has abandoned us. We think if God is good bad things shouldn't happen. How have you experienced God in your suffering?"

The overwhelming response was similar to Elena's, whose face lit up as she declared, "If it weren't for God's presence in my suffering, I wouldn't be alive!"

I pondered María's response. She said, "People who are bitter are often the ones who haven't suffered that much. Real suffering makes you realize the presence of God."

Recognizing God's presence in their suffering didn't mean they saw it as God's will. Pablo, an eighty-two-year-old villager, articulated the human cause of suffering. "God doesn't cause suffering," he explained. "Our suffering is because not everyone realizes we're all equal before God, members of one family. Big ones walk over little ones."

Pablo's understanding of suffering contrasted sharply with the displaced man in Cacaopera who saw himself as a disobedient child deserving God's punishment. Suffering was his fault, the result of his personal sin. The refugees, on the other hand, realized that suffering can also be caused by the sins of other people. They saw themselves as victims, the "little ones" walked on by those who don't recognize that God created everyone equal.

God's presence in the refugees' suffering didn't mean fatalistic resignation to it as God's will. Nor did it mean suffering was to be embraced as the way to find God. Suffering caused by disunity among people God created as equals was to be resisted. Resisting brought more suffering in the form of persecution and harassment—but it also brought the resisters closer to God. They found meaning in their hardship as they dedicated themselves to a cause.

I thought about another approach to suffering I had encountered. I vividly recalled a sermon given by an evangelical street preacher in Cacaopera's central plaza. The text was Luke 16. A rich man and Lazarus, a poor beggar, both die. But Lazarus goes to heaven while the rich man goes to hell.

"Lazarus sat at the gate day after day gratefully accepting whatever came his way," the preacher said. "He didn't complain. He didn't try to grab what he wanted from the rich man. And when he died, he received his heavenly reward."

I looked around at the people listening attentively. They were all poor. Several women had children in the nutrition program. The preacher went on to counsel them to accept their hardships with patience so that they, like Lazarus, would receive their heavenly reward. My heart cried out at what I was hearing. Everything I knew about God protested against passively accepting misery as the will of a just and loving God, to be alleviated only in the heavenly realm.

Three concepts of suffering were emerging. First, suffering as God's punishment for our personal sins. Second, suffering to be endured in this life in order to receive eternal life. Third, suffering because of broken relationships among God's people on earth.

My friend in Cacaopera who explained his hardship as God's punishment, and the evangelicals who accepted suffering in this life to earn their eternal reward, linked God's response directly to their actions. "If I'm bad, God will punish me. If I'm good, God will reward me." Their efforts to deal with suffering put God in a predictable, definable box.

But those who understood broken relationships among God's people as the cause of their hardships didn't view God as an authority figure meting out rewards and punishments. God was not the cause of their suffering. Nor was God merely present in their pain. God was actually suffering with them.

The thought that God suffers with us became important to me. I wrote down a quote by Thomas Merton.

Murder, massacres, revolution, hatred, the slaughter and torture of the bodies and souls of [human beings], the destruction of cities by fire, the starvation of millions, the annihila-
tion of populations and finally the cosmic inhumanity of
atomic war: Christ is massacred in His members, torn limb
from limb; God is murdered in [humanity].[13]

I was also struck by a statement made by a South African
priest, Albert Nolan. "Suffering makes God visible as the
one who is being sinned against."[14] Nolan summarized two
key concepts in one short sentence. First, God actually suffers with us. Second, we suffer not only because we are sin-
ners but also because we are sinned against. To sin against
others is to sin against God.

I was sobered by the thought that even now we crucify Jesus in our hatred, blindness, injustice, and violence. But if he
is still being crucified, he is also being raised from the dead.
Jesus' death and resurrection took on new meaning as I saw
it not only as a past, historical event, but also as ongoing reality.

The beginning of the rainy season always impressed me
as a symbolic demonstration of the life I sensed in the people around me. During the dry season, the countryside
looked like a scorched, barren desert. Fires started by ran-
dom bombing turned the hills into charred wasteland. But
after only one or two good rains, little green shoots would
begin to sprout. I was even inspired to write a poem.

Resurrection Triumphs

Gentle drops call forth life from earth's
   black coffin nailed shut by scorching sun,
     sealed by fire falling from the sky.

Thin wisps of green defy the tomb.

> Black boots stomp on tender new life.
>   Cruel heels grind the fresh face of hope
>   into the dirt.
>
> The steps pass
>   And the thin wisps of green lift their heads.

Nonviolence was another important issue, since being a pacifist in the middle of a war raised many questions. In Gotera I lived surrounded by government military forces. In Chalatenango I found myself in a region controlled by the FMLN rebels. What does it mean to be a pacifist identifying with people involved in a revolution?

I jotted down a quote by Arturo Paoli. "A revolution is like a cry, it's a problem opening up and spilling out on the floor right in front of everybody."[15] The image reminded me of an abscess that, left untreated, grows until the pus gathering beneath the surface finally spurts out. The abscess can't begin to heal until it ruptures.

I came to see that the violence in El Salvador didn't begin with the war. The revolution was like an abscess that burst from the pressure of social unrest. A rebel fighter described it this way. "Thousands of Salvadorans were killed before 1980 and no one paid attention. But as soon as the poor rose up in arms to put an end to their suffering, the whole world suddenly became concerned about violence in El Salvador. Violence existed before the war."

In July 1988 I attended a liberation theology course. A main speaker was Gustavo Gutiérrez, considered a founder of liberation theology. He said, "God is life. Poverty is death. Therefore we are committed to the poor." His statement rang true. Poverty kills people just like guns. I realized my understanding of nonviolence involved military violence but not the more subtle violence of oppressive structures.

I thought back to experiences in Gotera that taught me about the violence of poverty. Marta and Felícita came to mind. Some women from the church in Cacaopera told me that Marta's twelve-year-old daughter was severely malnourished. It seemed odd that a child that old would be malnourished, so I went to visit. As I approached the house, I called out a greeting but no one answered. I called again and went to the door. Now I saw a middle-aged woman grinding corn. She barely acknowledged my presence, unusual in the friendly Salvadoran society.

I explained I had come to see her daughter. She nodded toward a hammock. I looked and saw only blankets. Moving closer I noticed two huge eyes staring up at me from a skeletal face. I forced a smile and asked if I could lift the blankets. I was appalled at what I saw. Except for her bloated belly she was nothing but bones covered with a loose layer of skin. I put the blanket back and tried to gather my thoughts.

I asked Marta several questions. Her responses were brief and confusing. I managed to learn that the child had diarrhea and couldn't eat.

At that point a neighbor entered and told me their story. "Marta took the girl to the hospital when she first had diarrhea. It was a sacrifice because she barely had enough money for bus fare and the hospital fee. After waiting all morning, it was finally their turn to see the doctor.

"He glanced at the child, then scolded the mother. 'The girl doesn't even look sick. You're wasting my time. I have more important people to see than dirty Indians.' And he threw them out of his office.

"Now she refuses to go back to the hospital."

I turned to the mother. "It was unfair for the doctor to treat you that way. I'll go with you to the hospital. This time your daughter will receive treatment. If she doesn't go, she will die."

Marta wasn't convinced. Finally she said she didn't have time. "My husband died a month ago and I have to prepare for the forty-day mass."

My heart went out to her grief and loss. The woman loved her daughter but was engulfed by despair. She was considered the scum of the earth, poor, an Indian, a woman, displaced, no husband. Other efforts to convince her were fruitless. The girl died several days later, killed by the violence of poverty.

Felícita was another woman who introduced me to the violence of poverty. Every Sunday after church she would corner me, rambling on with a list of vague aches and pains. I would explain that I couldn't help her and she needed to go to the hospital.

She finally went. Three times she went—but never managed to see a doctor. By that time I realized I needed to become personally involved in her case. I learned she had given birth to eight children but seven had died in infancy. It sounded as if she had a prolapsed uterus (a complication of multiple pregnancies in which the uterus slips down through the vagina).

I helped her get an appointment with a doctor who examined her and scheduled her for surgery. Felícita had such poor self-esteem that when she got to the hospital she was too timid to talk to the receptionist. She explained to the cleaning woman that she had an appointment, but the cleaning woman told her the doctors were busy. So Felícita went home.

I was sorry I hadn't gone with her. The next week we went to the hospital together. We had to start all over again to get another appointment. It was one of my first experiences with the Salvadoran health care system; afterward I understood how she could go three times without seeing a doctor. We were jammed into a waiting room with about three hundred people. Shuffled from one line to another, we were out of luck if we didn't hear the nurses call her name.

We did finally see the doctor. He rescheduled the surgery but said we needed to find two blood donors first. We found two volunteers from her village, and I went with them to the blood bank. When we got there, they told us they couldn't take the blood because they didn't have blood bags. Since I was a foreigner with influence, I got bags from the Red Cross, an hour's drive away, and blood was drawn.

Felícita was admitted to the hospital and waited three days. Then she was told to go back home because the doctor was sick. She went home and returned later for the surgery. Felícita finally received treatment, but only because of my direct intervention and advocacy.

The experiences with Marta and Felícita would have been easier to understand if I could have written the doctors off as "bad people." But it wasn't that simple. Many doctors had their education interrupted for several years because the government closed the national university, accusing it of being a seedbed of communism. Classes resumed in 1985, but the department of medicine had been ransacked and didn't even have microscopes or books for the medical students.

After graduating from the university, interns are sent to rural hospitals for a year. Despite their inadequate university training, they work unsupervised. They attend a minimum of fifty outpatients a day and handle many other responsibilities. The doctor who saw Marta was probably tired, overworked, and poorly trained. There was no excuse for the way he treated her, but trying to understand his perspective put what happened in a different light.

I realized that good, well-meaning individuals make up violent structures that oppress the poor. Structural evil takes place because structures are more than a sum total of the individuals working within them. John Howard Yoder explains that God ordained structures to provide order and regularity. "But the structures fail to serve [people] as they should. They do not enable [one] to live a genuinely free, human, loving life. They have absolutized themselves and they demand from the individual and society an unconditional loyalty."[16]

Structures and the people within them sin against the poor in a way that makes it hard to identify who is responsible. Unable to pin the blame on others, I was forced to admit that I also shared responsibility for the violence of poverty. I was humbled as I recognized that simply refusing to bear arms didn't make me a good pacifist.

No matter how hard I try, I'm involved with structures that perpetuate violence and death. Eating bananas picked by underpaid workers in Honduras, I contribute to the deaths of their malnourished children. Drinking Salvadoran coffee, I perpetuate the exploitation of peasants who do the work while the landowners get rich. The contradictions can't be escaped. I feel called to nonviolence yet cannot extricate myself from violent structures.

It was helpful to identify the different types of violence around me—military, poverty, structural. But what was a faithful Christian response? I was struck several years ago by Vernard Eller's comparison of violence with whirlpools. The spiral of responding to violence with violence is like a whirlpool in a river. As the water pours in, it whirls faster and faster. The only way to stop the whirlpool is to place a solid rock in the middle. Peacemakers are called to be rocks in the whirlpool of violence. We're called to stand firm saying, "The violence stops here."

A personal experience with nonviolent confrontation in Las Vueltas kept my thoughts grounded in practice. There had been fighting in the hills for several days, and I spent two nights dozing fitfully on the floor as bombs fell and bullets flew. The second night the explosions were so close I was sure we would have injured villagers to care for in the clinic next morning.

After a night of constant gunfire, the morning silence was eerie. Looking out, I saw the soldiers sprawled outside the house. They had camouflage branches sticking out of their packs; their faces were painted grotesquely in green and black. They glared at me silently.

After a while I heard the noise of a helicopter landing nearby. Then I heard the rattle of chains and metal. Two huge German shepherd search dogs were being brought in to help with an intense house-to-house search. The soldiers dug up floors and yards, knocked down stone fences, and terrorized the villagers. Brandishing clubs, they told the people, "The guns are for the guerrillas and the clubs are for you."

By the end of the morning the "war material" soldiers had uncovered included the community typewriter, five watches, ten AM/FM radios, and scraps of tin from the tin workshop which they claimed was a bomb factory. They poured gasoline on the "goods" and made a bonfire.

At about 2:00 p.m. I heard noise outside our house and looked out to see a group of people forming. Mauricio, the village president, had been arrested and was being held across the street. Before long, about 150 people had gathered to demand his release.

I debated what my role should be. The initiative and responsibility belonged to the people but I wanted them to know I supported them. I decided to stand outside our house. This put me about three feet from the people but behind the line of soldiers.

Thoughts were hurling through my mind as I stood there. I felt a knot in my stomach as I watched the soldiers. They were obviously not the peasants forced into military service that I had often felt sorry for. These were hardened professionals enjoying the prospect of violence. They were excited, hungry for blood.

I had often wondered how human beings—husbands, sons, fathers—could commit massacres. How could they throw babies in the air and catch them on their bayonets? How could they slit open pregnant women and mutilate unborn children? But that afternoon I sensed I was in the presence of evil. I began to feel, if still not intellectually understand, the power evil wields.

The confrontation went on for two hours, with the crowd demanding Mauricio's release and the soldiers hurling back threats and accusations. Then the soldiers pulled out a camera. In a repressive country it is intimidating to think of your picture being circulated among the military. When the people saw the camera they tried to cover their faces with hats, hands, or arms. I understood their reaction but cringed to see them cower before evil. I hated seeing the soldiers' delight at the power they controlled in the form of a little black box.

Then I noticed Pablo. The 82-year-old Pablo was standing in the middle of the crowd, near the front. While those around him nervously tried to hide their faces, he stood calm and serene, looking the soldiers straight in the eye. He defied their power, daring them to take his picture, but it wasn't an angry, hateful challenge. He simply wasn't scared. Because the soldiers could not intimidate him, they held no power over him.

Tension mounted as men with machetes began milling around in back of the crowd. Then Angélica, Mauricio's wife, arrived, carrying their one-year-old grandson in her arms and holding their four-year-old daughter by the hand. She moved to the front of the jostling crowd and asked for her husband's release.

The soldiers responded by drawing a line in the dust. "We're not responsible for what happens to anyone who crosses this line," they declared.

Angélica demanded to see their commanding officer. They refused. Her body language communicated her internal struggle as she debated whether or not to push them further by crossing the line.

I was torn as I realized how badly I wanted the people to push to the limit, to show the power of courageous people standing firmly and nonviolently against injustice. I wanted them to be true to their values and not cower, to do what they had to in order to maintain their God-given dignity in the face of evil. But people could be killed or injured. Who was I to speak when standing safely on the sidelines? We were no longer talking about theory but lives.

Angélica made her decision. She stepped forward. She had barely taken a step when clubs started flying. I was mesmerized as I saw them beating twenty-year-old Cristina across the neck and shoulders. I felt Angélica run past me into the house while the children screamed in terror. The four-year-old had been clubbed in the forehead.

All that had barely registered when the sharp crack of gunfire split the air. Being a naive foreigner, I took the time to see if the soldiers were firing into the air or directly into the crowd. But the people, having been shot at in the past, immediately dove for cover. Since they were firing in the air I stayed where I was. My ears were ringing. I noticed with an absurd sense of clarity that the residue from the shots was filtering down, covering my blue skirt like ashes.

The shooting didn't last long. Pablo was one of the first to regain his composure. The colonel, having noticed his obvious place of influence and respect, called him over, hoping Pablo would convince the people to go home.

Pablo listened respectfully and went back to the milling crowd. "The colonel says you should go home," he said, as he took his place once more. Then, as a father scolds a naughty child, he calmly reprimanded the soldiers for misusing their power against innocent civilians.

By that time it was almost dark. When the officer declared a state of siege and threatened to shoot anyone on the streets, the crowd dispersed. Mauricio was released the next morning.

I didn't know Pablo well before that incident, but I was anxious to talk to him. He was surely an example of nonviolent resistance, a "rock in the middle of a whirlpool." I asked him how he felt during the confrontation.

"When we think we can't keep going, God gives us his hand and his Spirit to continue," he replied. "I wasn't scared because I'm ready to die." Then he told me of four different occasions when he came close to death but his strong will to live pulled him through.

It struck me that Pablo could be a rock in the midst of violence because he was ready to die at the same time as he fought to live. I was reminded of 1 John 3:16: "This is how we know what love is: Jesus Christ laid down his life for us. And we ought to lay down our lives for our [sisters and] brothers." Love turns our natural instincts to protect and preserve our own lives into willingness to die for the sake of our friends.

Trying to apply my beliefs about nonviolence was humbling. Theoretical discussions can allow us the illusion that we're willing to sacrifice our lives to be peacemakers—but practical experience shattered any heroic fantasies. I had experienced two similar confrontations with soldiers when they had arrested villagers. Both times I was faced with questions about my involvement. "What is my role as a foreigner? Is this situation worth dying for? Is nonviolent resistance at this time, in this way, what God is calling me to do?" I wished the issues were clear but they were always murky.

If I was going to die a peacemaker, then I wanted it to be worthwhile. Surely if I knew my death could concretely save someone's life, I would be willing to die. My death would even be a testimony of nonviolent resistance. But my limited experience made me wonder if a "worthwhile death" was an illusion. It seemed more likely that I could be killed under vague circumstances, leaving outsiders wondering if I had thrown my life away due to poor judgment or to confusion about Christianity and politics.   *

While peacemakers debate when to die for the sake of nonviolent intervention, soldiers die every day for the sake of violent responses to conflict. I had nothing to say to the

Marxist combatant who asked, "Why are Christians who believe in life after death less willing to die than we humanists?
You would think we who believe this life is the end would
be less willing to sacrifice it than Christians, but that hasn't
been my experience."

The combination of reflection and experience didn't provide solutions, but did clarify several personal issues. First,
only God's grace could enable me to respond appropriately
and nonviolently during a crisis. Second, I had been arro-
gant in saying, "Peacemakers must be as willing to die for
nonviolent change as soldiers are to die in war." Profound
statements lose their power when glibly repeated with little
understanding of the commitment involved. Third, I had
judged those who took up arms without understanding the
violence that drove them to it.

Becoming more aware of the pervasiveness of violence
took a toll on my emotions. In February 1989 I wrote a pas-
sionate journal entry as I realized how the tenacious roots of
violence find their way into every aspect of life.

> I hate violence. I hate it. I hate the way it makes people mis-
> trust each other. I hate the way it plays into people's weak-
> ness for power and money. I hate its arrogance. I hate the
> way it forces good, kind people to respond to it in equally evil
> fashion. I hate the way it makes people lie and deceive each
> other, the divisions it causes. I hate violence, not just the war.
> The war isn't the cause of the violence, it's the response.

I was upset as I saw how violence breeds mistrust. The
community where I lived was not immune to problems
stemming from a lack of trust, even though the people were
dedicated to working together. Nor was I immune to the af-
fects of violence on personal relationships. My reaction to
stress and tension often prevented me from responding sen-
sitively to people I cared about.

12

Wounded, Re-wounded, Exhausted

By the end of 1988, I had decided to continue indefinitely in El Salvador. The first several months after reaching an open-ended commitment to living in Chalatenango, I experienced only the benefits. I could dream about the future of the health work. I could celebrate the small steps toward long range goals without the pressure of wanting to accomplish objectives before the end of my term. Most important, relationships deepened as friends sensed we would be together over the long haul. I was not prepared, however, for the pain that came from my relationships as people I loved were killed, captured, and victimized by Salvadoran government forces.

After a long series of human rights abuses, I wrote in my journal,

> What does it mean to embrace a theology that results in wounding and re-wounding? I can't share the lives of the people in a significant way and blithely say I know God has called me to live here because this is a healthy place for me.
> I know God has called me here. Not because this is where

I experience just enough challenge to make me grow. But because this is where I feel hurt and overwhelmed, where I'm tottering on the brink of trust and faith, doubt and weakness, yet have no desire to leave because of assurance that this is where my heart is.

During 1989, harassment against our work occurred almost every month. In January, five co-workers were arrested as we initiated a vaccination campaign against childhood diseases. An MCC couple with their six-month-old baby were placed under house arrest for accompanying a group of health promoters who came to seek the release of their companions. In February, $3,000 worth of medicines we had painstakingly bought and packed were confiscated by the military. Our efforts to get them back were fruitless. Soldiers searched our clinic in March and publicly accused the health workers of collaborating with the guerrillas. They also confiscated two boxes of dental supplies.

April brought more harassment against the vaccination efforts. Despite a nationwide measles epidemic, the army refused to allow the International Red Cross to vaccinate in Las Vueltas. I found my teeth clenched in anger as clods of dirt fell on two-year-old Jessica's coffin. She had needlessly died of measles because the army refused her a simple vaccine.

Then there was Anabel, denied two basic rights—the right to be vaccinated and the right to medical care. Her mother took her to the hospital emergency room ill with measles. The doctor wrote a prescription for Tylenol without even looking at the child. Anabel was admitted to the hospital only after her mother went back accompanied by a North American doctor. She died the next day.

On April 22, members of the church health program performed vaccinations in our parish. Soldiers in one village warned parents not to allow their children to receive the "guerrilla vaccine." As a result, we vaccinated twelve children. Over eighty had received the first dose the month before.

I thought about Jesus' love for children and about the recent needless deaths. Writing to a friend, I said,

> Anyone who wages war against little children is my enemy. Having admitted it, I suddenly find myself struggling with hate. What does it mean to "love my enemy"?
>
> But even as I struggle with hate, I recognize that I've learned to love more. And as I struggle with the ugliness of evil I have a deeper appreciation for the beauty of good. I guess the painfulness of the struggle isn't too high a price to pay to stop being lukewarm.

The incidents continued. Two health promoters from Las Vueltas were arrested at the end of April. One was beaten. In May, the MCC country directors were denied entrance into El Salvador because their names were on a list of unwelcome people. A foreign doctor responsible for the dental programs was expelled in July, and about $30,000 worth of medicine destined for the whole diocese was confiscated. Most of the medicines were finally returned after intense international pressure.

The same day the medicines were confiscated, another kind of tragedy occurred. Victoria, a close Salvadoran friend from Gotera, was killed in a car accident. Living in an isolated area, I didn't find out about her death until it was too late to go to the funeral. My emotional turmoil continued until I was able to visit Gotera several weeks later.

In August a foreign co-worker was threatened by a death squad. In September six health promoters were detained on their way to one of our courses. One was interrogated for four hours because soldiers found a diagram in his notebook describing the transmission of infectious diseases by water, excrement, and flies. They claimed the triangle with arrows was a code for a guerrilla attack.

During those months I drew strength from Carlo Caretto's description of the traditional celebration of lights. Gazing at candles, the participants repeat, "This candle is the symbol of Jesus who gives light to the world by being consumed as this candle is being consumed." I wrote,

> A light is shining in the darkness of El Salvador. From a distance it is a beautiful symbol of hope. But from up close one realizes that its warm, flickering glow is fueled by the tortured flesh of Salvadorans willing to die for the sake of their sisters and brothers. The light of hope is dependent on those willing to be consumed by suffering and death.

At the same time, I realized that there were many undramatic ways of being consumed. There were my struggles with guarding my time and space, responding ungraciously to interruptions, and my deeply rooted individualism. God was calling me to lay myself down freely and compassionately in the mundane, nitty-gritty of daily life.

The roots of the tension I felt, however, were deeper than the human rights abuses in themselves. My tension had to do with the realization that not only were the soldiers my enemies but I was theirs. I was working with people from repopulated communities who were committed to promoting social change. The military was threatened by the fact that the same people forced to flee in the early '80s had returned empowered by unity and vision. Identifying with them made me the army's enemy.

The military considered anyone working in the repopulation communities to be leftists connected to the FMLN and thus did everything possible to restrict access to rural conflictive areas. They asked church officials to withdraw pastoral workers, demanded military safe conduct passes which they refused to grant, and made it difficult for foreigners to renew residency visas.

While our lives weren't in obvious danger, the underlying

tension was stressful. Church officials didn't ask us to leave, but at times we felt unsupported in our efforts to stay. Foreigners were turned back at the military checkpoint on the way to Chalatenango because we didn't have military permission. But those who had applied were turned down anyway, so we were forced to begin leaving San Salvador at 3:30 a.m. to pass military checkpoints before the soldiers were awake. The night before I would find myself tense and uptight, unable to sleep as I wondered if we would make it back. Instead of a relaxing break from work, trips to San Salvador became an energy-draining chore.

Even though I was convinced we were right not to allow the military to determine where we worked, I still felt twinges of guilt driving down the abandoned road in the middle of the night. Was I sneaking around in the darkness defying government authorities ordained by God? Or was I faithfully "obeying God rather than humans"?

Political tensions were mounting during the beginning of 1989; rumors of an insurrection were rampant. The escalating conflict polarized the situation, forcing people to identify with one side or the other. There was no room for neutrality; I felt the need to define my position more clearly. What did it mean to take sides? Are not Christians called to be neutral reconcilers in the midst of conflict?

A pamphlet by Albert Nolan, a South African priest, was helpful. Nolan proposes that Christians are indeed called to take sides in certain kinds of conflict. He identifies three misperceptions in the position that being a peacemaker always means reconciling two opposing forces.

First, the position of reconciliation assumes that the conflict is based on misunderstandings that can be cleared up by facilitating communication. But in some conflicts there is a right side and wrong side. Christians aren't called to try to reconcile good and evil, justice and injustice. We are called to do away with evil and injustice.

Second, the reconciliation position assumes that a person can be neutral. But in cases of injustice and oppression, neutrality is impossible. If we don't side with the oppressed, we automatically side with the oppressor by consciously or unconsciously maintaining the status quo.

Third, the position that Christians should always seek reconciliation and harmony assumes that tension and conflict are worse evils than injustice and oppression.

Nolan writes that "truth and justice must be promoted at all costs, even at the cost of creating conflict and dissension along the way."[17] Jesus was clear. "Do you think I came to bring peace on earth? No, I tell you, but division." Jesus did not want to cause division. But his uncompromising stance inevitably divided the people into those who were for him and those who were against him.

The conflict in El Salvador was clearly due to injustice which I had to denounce, not reconcile. The area where I lived was controlled by the rebels. They were also denouncing injustice but trying to overthrow the government through violence. How should I relate to them in light of the biblical mandate to submit to the government as ordained by God?

Romans 13 presents governing authorities as God's servants for doing good, as rulers who hold no terror for those who do right. Are we called to submit when the tables are turned and the government persecutes those who do right? As a local cooperative member said, "Even doing good is prohibited (by the military)." The people in my area had chosen the revolutionary movement as their legitimate authority. I struggled with my position.

My experience indicated that the revolutionary government was a more just authority than the legally recognized Salvadoran government. The church's role of calling government to justice was relatively easy with the rebel leaders, who encouraged dialogue. Voicing opinions to the Salvadoran government and military officials, however, meant risking persecution, harassment, and possible death.

I came to recognize that, in a civil war, there can be two governing authorities. The church's role in calling government to justice is constant. But how we are received in that role determines to what extent the government and the church can work together.

It was helpful to clarify my thoughts, but my emotions still clamored for attention. We had no idea what would happen if the war escalated. But if it did, repercussions against the repopulated communities were all but certain. I struggled against being swept away by rumors but wanted to be realistic about the fact that I could be killed or injured. In February I wrote a letter to a friend.

> The significance of Ash Wednesday struck me with force. What will the next forty days in the desert bring? Will someone find my journal and read what I was thinking and feeling just before "the end"? How real is the possibility of dying?
>
> My heart is heavy with foreboding. My friends have made a commitment. What does it mean to accompany them? Will Mennonites write me off as having gotten carried away by politics?
>
> A crisis is imminent. I feel more confident about being faithful in a short-term crisis than in my ability to be faithful in the long run. I have a feeling that this is going to be a long-term endurance test. The obstacles are wearing, eating away at my energy little by little.

My commitment to nonviolence stimulated me to look for creative ways of resisting. I thought seriously about how to respond nonviolently to the harassment we experienced in our health work. The seeds of a dream had been planted in Gotera when I wished the victims of inadequate medical attention would voice their protests. That dream began to be fulfilled in Chalatenango.

Truth had been an important theme to me for several years. Now Isaiah 59:14-15 caught my attention. "Truth has stumbled in the streets, honesty cannot enter. Truth is nowhere to be found, and whoever shuns evil becomes a prey."

To speak the truth about injustice is to participate with God in upholding the cause of righteousness. Taking the prophetic call to denounce injustice seriously, we formed a commission to document abuses suffered by the poor in the health care system, the harassment of health workers, and the bombing of civilians. The commission not only wrote reports but also organized to respond to emergencies. At least the promoters would have the support of public pressure as a nonviolent backup system for the risks they were taking to serve their communities.

The army's harassment of health workers was intended to intimidate them into quitting. Anger, frustration, and fear are powerful emotions that can either destroy or make us stronger. Albert Nolan writes, "A love that is vigorous, determined, and effective is an angry love. Anger must not be nursed, it must be transformed into drive, energy, determination, creativity, and courage."[18] Having an organized way for the promoters to respond to harassment was a way of transforming anger into a constructive force.

I was also concerned about revealing why the church had become involved in providing health care. Promoting church-run health programs without unmasking the inadequacies of the government health care system temporarily bailed out the government. It did not promote a long-term solution. Denouncing the government without providing alternative health care left the poor suffering without even the most basic health services. The church programs I was familiar with were better at providing health care than pointing out the injustice that made it necessary for the church to intervene.

The intensity of the situation forced me to live in the present. Dealing with the past becomes a luxury when surviving the present demands all of one's energy. Planning for the future seems irrelevant to people who don't know if they will be alive tomorrow. I found it difficult to distance myself enough to prepare for the two-month speaking tour that was to begin the end of October.

My speaking commitment weighed heavily on me for several reasons. I was emotionally and physically exhausted. I was running on reserve energy and didn't know how long it would last. I knew from previous speaking engagements that I was capable of communicating effectively, but it took a great deal of energy for me to exercise my extroverted side.

I was pleased that so many MCC regions wanted me to speak. But the full schedule overwhelmed me. I decided to retreat before starting. Those five days of rejuvenation got me through the first three weeks. But nothing could have adequately prepared me to cope with what followed.

The FMLN launched a military offensive several weeks after I began speaking; the psychological impact left my energy reserves depleted. There was so much—worry about friends who were being arrested, expelled, or killed. Questions about what was happening in the rural areas. Grief at the assassination of six Jesuit priests (two of whom I knew personally) and two women. Concern about the MCCers and the fact that our offices had been ransacked. Anger and frustration at my impotence.

I simply reached the end of my endurance. Even though it was an ideal time to speak about El Salvador since interest was high, I had to admit I couldn't continue.

After canceling my commitments, I headed for a camp in the Cascade mountains, where I did nothing but sleep the first twenty-four hours. It was good that I was somewhat rested when the ham radio message came that my father was in the hospital with a brain tumor.

13

Struggle and Hope

The camp I had gone to was accessible only by a boat which made the trip every other day. The radio message that Dad was to have brain surgery Monday came Saturday night. Fortunately the boat was coming the following day.

Meanwhile, about twelve inches of snow had fallen, the first snow of the season. Surrounded by majestic mountains blanketed by new-fallen snow, I found it hard to comprehend that my father could be seriously ill. Sunday morning I went cross-country skiing as I waited for the boat. At 1:00 p.m. I began the long journey from Washington state to Ohio.

I called several friends while I waited for my 1:00 a.m. flight, then sat alone in the airport restaurant writing in my journal. I felt battered, still reeling from one blow when the next hit with force. I clung to the solitude of anonymity in the airport, correctly sensing that I needed to take advantage of the transition time. It was November 26, 1989. I mentally reviewed the previous month.

It had been exactly four weeks since I had started speaking in San José, California. Averaging two or three presentations a day, I had traveled in California, Oregon, Michigan, Alberta, and British Columbia.

On Sunday evening, November 12, word that the heaviest fighting of the war had broken out in San Salvador absorbed my emotional energy. I had a free evening and was alone in the house where I was staying, quietly preparing myself for the busy week ahead. The one-minute news report about El Salvador shattered my calm. Worried and frustrated, I tried to call the MCCers in San Salvador but couldn't get a line. I slept fitfully that night before flying the next day to Calgary, Alberta.

Fighting in El Salvador dominated the news for the next week. I cried tears of frustration at not being able to accompany the people I cared about during the time they needed support. "I know nothing I could do would make a difference if I were there," I said in numerous phone calls to MCC headquarters. "But I want to go back as soon as possible. We talk so much about 'accompaniment.' What is it if not being present even in our impotence and helplessness?"

By the end of the week I was hopeful about going back soon. But the director of MCC suddenly put a damper on my enthusiasm. After all, we had identified education in North America as one of our priorities. Speaking while El Salvador was on the news was an ideal opportunity. Knowing he was right didn't help my crushed emotions. But it was Dad's reaction that took me aback. Always supportive of whatever I felt I needed to do, this time he clearly did not want me to leave sooner than I had planned. I knew I needed to listen.

The decision was still mine. No one was giving me orders. The next morning I was to start a week of engagements in British Columbia. I had the afternoon at a friend's house in Bellingham, Washington, to decide what to do. God didn't seem to hear my prayers begging the doors for my return to open. Instead, I was realizing I could face fear better than impotence. Anything was better than the frustration of helplessness. And theoretically, I believed in listening to the counsel of other people. I couldn't go back against the advice of my family and MCC.

Having reached that conclusion, I could begin to feel the exhaustion I had been fighting for most of a year. It would be foolish to walk into the midst of a crisis physically and emotionally depleted. I even began to wonder if I had the energy for another month of speaking. I tried to push the question out of my mind. I had made the commitment knowing it was a heavy schedule. It was too late to back out. Besides, I wasn't a quitter. I would just have to push harder. It was the least I could do for the people of El Salvador.

I thought about my emotions and wondered how close I was to the nebulous "breaking point." I wasn't sleeping at night and my hands would periodically shake so hard I could hardly hold a cup. But it was easier to blame others. I felt as if MCC was asking too much of me by planning an eight-week schedule without even one day off a week. Until I stood up for myself, there had been a three-week stretch without one free day. People sometimes fall between the cracks even of good, caring institutions like MCC. Church institutions are not immune from the structural tendency to dehumanize.

No one was intentionally asking more than I could give. It was my responsibility to recognize when the personal toll was becoming too great. I chose to stop speaking. The caring, compassionate reaction from everyone involved confirmed that my respect for MCC was well-placed.

My musings were interrupted as an El Salvador news report about a friend, Jennifer Casolo, flashed on the airport TV screen. Arrested and accused by the Salvadoran military of hiding arms for the guerrillas, Jennifer had captured the hearts of many North Americans during her two-week ordeal. My mind flitted back and forth between El Salvador, speaking, and my father.

Thoughts of Dad's impending surgery dominated the last

leg of my journey. I arrived at the hospital an hour before the operation. Anxious for details, I learned he had had a spell on Saturday during which his right side had suddenly become paralyzed. Thinking he was having a stroke, they rushed him to the hospital. A CAT scan revealed a large brain tumor.

Other than the fact that I had never seen him in a hospital bed, Dad looked normal to me. Surely nothing could be seriously wrong. But the doctor and he had had a long private talk. We never knew exactly what passed between them, but Dad was obviously prepared for a difficult outcome. He motioned me over to his side. The words he spoke are indelibly imprinted on my heart.

"I still stand by the decision you made to go to Bolivia when Mother was sick," he said. "We told you then that we dedicated you to God when you were a baby and we meant it. I want to affirm that again.

"You have a call from God that you must follow. Some people may think that because you're single you should change your plans to be with me if necessary, but I don't want that. I only ask that you let me be emotional when you leave without thinking the tears mean I'm not willing to let go of you."

Tears welled up as we embraced, but I was too overwhelmed by conflicting emotions—gratefulness, fear, love, sorrow, pain—even to begin expressing them. Five or six people were in the room, witnesses of my father's blessing. Always my supporter and defender, even then he was protecting me from dealing with the burden of other people's expectations, lovingly freeing me to serve where I felt called. I wondered if he had purposely spoken with others present so there could be no doubt as to his wishes.

But the stretcher was waiting outside the room. We gathered around his bed to pray before they took him. During the next four hours of waiting, I experienced peace based not on expectation that the outcome would be positive according to our definitions but on trust that God was with us.

There were probably six or eight of us in the waiting room when the surgeon entered. Even now my chest tightens as I recall the impact of his words. ". . . a large, aggressive, malignant tumor in the dominant part of the brain . . . impossible to get it all . . . only time will tell how much function he will recover."

I took several deep breaths trying to loosen the band that felt as if it were constricting my heart and lungs. I could think only of the slow, tortuous struggle looming before us. Was it an advantage or disadvantage to have already lost one parent to cancer and have an idea what to expect? Few tears found their way up from my heart. Survival had demanded that I suppress them for too long.

Even though Daddy had given his blessing for me to return to El Salvador, I debated what I should do. Taking a year to be with him seemed to make sense until I took the situation in El Salvador into account. Then I would think I couldn't possibly stay away. After all, Dad had the support of loving family and friends as well as the best of medical science. He would appreciate having me close but the greater need was in El Salvador. I decided to return at the end of January as originally planned.

The following days were a haze of fitful nights sleeping on the ICU waiting room floor, visitors coming and going, telephone calls, and most of all, waiting. Waiting, waiting, always waiting, just like with Mother. For what? Waiting to see if he would be able to move his right side. Waiting for indications that he might regain his speech. Waiting for the pathology report. Waiting for him to be moved to the rehabilitation floor. The days of waiting turned into weeks. Waiting for Daddy to come home. Waiting for the radiation treatments to finish. Waiting for the next CAT scan. Waiting for symptoms that the tumor was growing.

To live with waiting. It's a paradox. Waiting for the future tends to overpower living in the present. But even in dying Dad taught me how to live. He was depressed around his sixty-fifth birthday in December. He had been looking forward to retiring so he and Donna could do voluntary service. But his dreams for the future were smashed. He had to grieve them before he could move on. Once he did that, he could experience the richness of each day in and of itself. Many people never reach that point.

"Enduring hope is not something innate, something we possess from birth," the German theologian, Jurgen Moltmann says. "Nor do we acquire it by experience. We have to learn it."[19] He explains that we learn to hope by obeying the call to stand our ground against death and despair. To despair is to give up, to stop trying. It leads to hopelessness.

Even while accepting the inevitability of his death, my father needed to resist it to live out his last days with hope and meaning. Salvadorans willing to die so that their children might have a better future were also learning hope by standing against the despair threatening to destroy them. Dorothee Soelle, another German theologian, expresses it this way: "Struggle is the source of hope. There is no hope without struggle."[20]

The pain of the people of El Salvador was so present in my heart I couldn't process my father's illness without integrating it with the pain of my suffering friends. I felt isolated in my processing, separated from my friends in El Salvador and still unable to articulate my pain in a way that those who had never experienced the injustice of oppression could understand. I didn't write much in my journal during those weeks but what I did write was significant.

> I react against those who act as if what is happening to our family is the worst thing in the world that could possibly happen. Yes, it's sad and painful, but what about the people who

are cut down in their prime because of the lack of medical care or war or repression; people who have never had the opportunity to grow and develop because they are poor and die anonymously?

I thought, too, about miracles. Were we in danger of missing the miracles God was performing by defining miracle as "supernatural healing"?

> Pablo said, "For those who trust in God, no ground is barren." A piece of myself died the moment the doctor said the tumor was malignant and they didn't get it all. Is that piece dead, wasted, gone forever? Or will it be like a seed that falls to the ground and dies, thereby producing many seeds?
>
> Even as we pray for miraculous healing, I ask myself if God could work anything more miraculous than transforming the death that is at work in each of us into life; transforming suffering into perseverance, character, and hope. Hope cannot come out of anything as evil as suffering unless God is alive and active, creating what was meant to destroy us into maturity and strength.

In the same journal entry I wrote about the interconnectedness of suffering. Again I recalled Pablo's words, rooted in wisdom he had learned from life experience. "Our suffering is because not everyone realizes that we are equal before God. The big ones walk all over the little ones."

But the consequences of the intertwining web of connections aren't all negative. I also experienced the fact that living interconnectedly as God intended is enabling. I could go to Bolivia while Mother was dying because others in my family and church assumed responsibilities I otherwise would have had. My father was now enabling me to continue working in El Salvador by allowing God to meet his needs through others. And the many people supporting him enabled him to let go of me with the confidence that he wasn't alone.

I returned to El Salvador on January 24. Leaving my father was painful. But I was strengthened by God's presence and leading.

I wasn't sure what to expect after the turmoil caused by the offensive and was anxious about what I would find. My papers and personal belongings in San Salvador were in amazingly good shape considering the way the National Guard had ransacked the house, dumping out files and strewing clothes, books, pictures all over the floor.

They had then thrown our belongings into big garbage bags which they carted off to their headquarters. Thanks to the persistence of the MCCers, most of what had been taken was returned (along with an interesting assortment of miscellaneous items from other ransacked houses).

I received a wonderful homecoming walking into Las Vueltas after three months away. "This is clearly home," I wrote. "People love and accept me even when I fail to live up to my own expectations and have trouble accepting myself." It took three hours to walk the two blocks from the edge of town to my room as people eagerly greeted me and filled me in on the news.

Soon after I returned, I helped vaccinate in Corral de Piedra, the latest community resettled by former Mesa Grande refugees. Little did I know that less than two weeks later air force helicopters and planes would rocket the village—killing five, four of whom were children, and injuring fifteen. I arrived soon after the bombing, as villagers literally scraped the last strips of mutilated flesh off the floor and walls and closed the caskets.

The next day I took advantage of a quick ride to San Salvador to call home. The news hit hard. Dad had been in the hospital for a week with pneumonia. I had forgotten about the jolt of news from home when so much is at stake.

On our way back to Chalatenango the next day, the soldiers detained us at a checkpoint from 7:30 a.m. until 3:30

p.m. By the time I arrived in Las Vueltas I was feeling frenzied and harried.

The following weeks were busy but positive. Meanwhile, word came that Dad wasn't recuperating well from the pneumonia. Although absorbed by the intensity of daily life, I found myself periodically thrust brusquely back into my other reality. My heart would race every time a jeep unexpectedly pulled into Las Vueltas. Was it Cathy, a friend and co-worker, bringing news about my father?

Thursday afternoon, April 11, I was sitting in my room finishing last-minute preparations for a health course that was to start Sunday. When I heard a truck, I looked up and saw the community's pickup pass with two hammocks hung in the back. My heart sank. Someone was sick or injured. I hurried to the clinic.

Several men from a neighboring village had found a grenade when they were fishing. Thinking it was a dud, one man hit it with a machete; it exploded. He was killed and three others were injured. Eighteen-year-old Teodoro's injuries were serious. One eye was clearly beyond saving and the other so swollen it was hard to tell.

Hours from medical care, over washed-out roads, we were fortunate a doctor from the FMLN was able to provide emergency care. He gave Teodoro two units of blood and operated on his eye. By next morning it appeared Teodoro would recover without complications, but when he took his first sips of water, he went into shock. The shrapnel injuries on his abdomen looked like mere scratches, but a piece could have penetrated. The doctor operated and found two holes in his stomach. The emergency operation saved his life but he needed to be hospitalized as soon as possible.

It was 4:30 p.m. by the time a hammock was strung in the back of the pickup and we started the five-hour trip to San Salvador. The road never felt so long or bumpy. I wondered if Teodoro would survive the trip. It was 9:45 p.m. when we arrived at the first army checkpoint. As soon as the soldiers realized our patient was a young man, they accused us of transporting a wounded guerrilla and detained us almost two hours. Teodoro's tortuous breathing echoed in my ears. Finally they let us continue, but then it started raining. I wondered what else could happen. I soon found out.

We arrived at the hospital emergency room at 1:00 a.m. Good Friday morning. No sooner had we pulled in than we were swarmed by National Police officers. Evidently soldiers at the checkpoint had radioed ahead to say we were coming. Fortunately, the emergency room staff insisted on giving Teodoro immediate medical attention, so at least he was being taken care of while his father and I were interrogated by the police.

The accusations, while unspoken, were clearly communicated. Teodoro was a young man injured by a grenade. Thus he had to be a guerrilla. I was a guerrilla sympathizer because I brought him in for medical care. The fact that he had been operated on by a guerrilla doctor confirmed their suspicions. The police said they were placing Teodoro under custody. We notified the International Red Cross the following morning and went back to the hospital, where Teodoro was recuperating nicely from another operation.

Fortunately, Teodoro's story ended happily. The police eventually left him alone and he recuperated with only the loss of one eye.

On April 26 I received a note to call home as soon as possible. I was in the town of Chalatenango, so I called from there. After a frustrating hour-and-a-half wait for the call to go through, I learned Dad had pneumonia again and the tumor was growing. Since I had been planning a trip home in May, I changed the date and went two weeks earlier.

By the time I arrived, Dad had pulled through the crisis and was much better. Our last month together was special. Realizing that I didn't have the facts straight on stories of his life I had grown up hearing, I asked if he would be interested in my writing them down. He responded enthusiastically.

And so we spent hours talking and reviewing old photo albums. We also discussed his funeral and other difficult subjects that I hadn't been ready to face before I left in January. Our understanding when I returned to El Salvador in May was that I would try to get back again before he died but he wouldn't hang on for my sake.

"I struggle with wishing the dying process wasn't so long on the one hand and savoring each day as a gift on the other," I wrote. Watching my father helped me savor each moment. Yes, it was hard being an invalid, sitting day after day in a chair, working at physical therapy despite the certainty of fighting a losing battle, being dependent, letting go of his dreams. Yet it was spring and he enjoyed the birds, chose which flowers to plant, and discussed the garden. Who was I to say the quality of his life wasn't worth the struggle?

Living with the certainty of our finiteness enriches the present. The illusion that we are in control of our own destiny drives us. Maintaining the pretense of self-sufficiency saps our energy. When the illusions are shattered and the pretenses drop, we are freed to embrace what life offers.

I saw this in my father. I see it in my Salvadoran friends. The death threatening them resurrects in newness of life. As the Salvadoran Jesuit theologian, Jon Sobrino, said in an interview, "[The oppressed] don't take life for granted. For those of us who take life for granted, life cannot be an object of hope. . . . In the presence of death, life itself makes sense."[21]

Dad's condition deteriorated during my last week at home and the day before my departure I was still debating if I should leave. "I can't get away from the extremes," I wrote. "Right now I'm so close to the situation that I can almost drive myself crazy wondering if there is really a change from day to day or if such and such a symptom is significant. When I leave I will be at the opposite extreme of not knowing anything. I dread being isolated again."

I finally decided what I had in the past. Dad had other help available. He didn't need me to make sure he received quality care.

Back in Las Vueltas, I was touched by the compassion people demonstrated as I shared about my father's illness. They didn't belittle my pain by measuring it against their own. They had suffered enough to know that comparisons were irrelevant.

I still hadn't learned that yet years before when I talked to my dad about suffering. According to an article I had just read, "real" suffering stems from oppression. Other experiences may be painful but aren't suffering.

Dad's response left my intellectual distinctions flapping uselessly. "I suffered when Mother died," he declared, his voice trembling with emotion.

He said nothing more. But I knew I was wrong in allowing intellectual fine points to interfere with compassion.

Chenta asked about my father one morning at breakfast. We talked about my struggles and then the conversation naturally shifted to hers. We shared deeply and genuinely.

"When I'm home alone, I often spend the whole day crying," she said with tears in her eyes.

A thirty-two-year-old North American grieving her father's impending death and a forty-five-year-old Salvadoran peasant grieving the loss of her husband and children found a common core in the depths of our pain.

At MCC meetings in July we read a challenging article about missions. How do we live incarnationally among those we are called to serve? Jesus called the rich young ruler to give up his financial security in favor of the security offered by a community of disciples. What did that say to us?

"We are called to cast our lot with the poor, which doesn't

imply that we are exactly like them," a friend commented. "It means that we put our energy and resources at their disposal."

Those discussions prepared the ground for an unexpected milestone in my life. On July 19 I made a vow to cast my lot with the poor. Seventeen health promoters were my witnesses. This is what happened.

I was participating in a basic training course for new health workers. One of our classes dealt with the link between malnutrition and poverty, so we started the day by giving four of the participants a special breakfast of fried beans, eggs, cheese, and milk. The rest received plain beans and tortillas.

The outcome was startling. Initially, no one said anything. It seemed they hadn't noticed. Then one of the promoters with the special plate suddenly realized not everyone had what she had. She immediately passed her plate around, almost begging the others to share her food.

They politely refused, not at all upset to be eating the plain beans and tortillas that they would eat everyday at home. But the woman with the special breakfast paced the floor, increasingly agitated by her position. The other three ate the food in total silence. I thought the discussion was going to flop.

After breakfast, we began the day's classes. We were to start with some preliminary announcements, but the short time between breakfast and the session had been enough to get the words flowing. It became clear that nothing could take precedence over discussing the unusual breakfast. I looked around the room. One of the four had her head on her desk and was refusing to speak.

"Someone called her rich," her neighbor explained. Being called rich is an insult among the poor, who link wealth with injustice and selfishness. Another of the four, Lencho, was nowhere to be found. A coordinator went to look for him and came back saying he was in the street crying and re-fused to come back to the class.

Lencho was about eighteen, a new promoter I didn't know well. I went to talk to him. "It wasn't fair what you did," he said, with tears streaming down his face. "You had no right to give some people more than others. If there wasn't enough good food you should have divided whatev-er there was in equal parts. It wasn't fair."

What I thought would simply be a discussion starter was taking an unexpected turn. I explained that it was just a way of getting the group to talk about nutrition and poverty. The words sounded empty even to me.

"You don't know how much I've suffered," he said. "I grew up an orphan in the street watching other people eat good food while I struggled to survive. I wouldn't have been upset if I had been given just beans and tortillas but I didn't deserve the good breakfast. It wasn't fair for me to have the special food. How can I go back in and face the group, know-ing I didn't deserve what I got?"

We talked for thirty minutes and the tears never stopped. He didn't sob in anger or frustration. Nor was it a good cry that finally expressed bottled-up feelings. The tears just flowed as if the experience had tapped a well of pain that could be plugged but never dried. I was overwhelmed by the rawness of his heart and his deep sense of unworthiness. I wondered what I had done.

As I sat with him I remembered a friend's account of an experience during MCC orientation. Two people were giv-en a special dinner, a larger group was given something plain, and the rest ate rice. It happened that one who re-ceived the special dinner had been quite poor, forced to scrape bottom as she struggled to raise her family. But her response was quite different from Lencho's. Her reaction was that she had suffered enough; it was about time the ta-bles turned, allowing her to enjoy good food.

I wished Lencho could show a similar recognition of justice. Instead, he continued to repeat, "I didn't deserve it. I didn't deserve it." Injustice destroys its victims from within and without. It forces them into a trap and convinces them it's what they deserve. Even when the outer walls are removed, people like Lencho feel so unworthy that they fatalistically accept their plight as God's will.

Lencho's lack of self-dignity and pride as a human being created in God's image ran so deep that he couldn't even accept a gift of grace as small as a good breakfast. How could I respond? I found myself moving from a sense of guilt for having touched his wound to anger at the position society had forced him into.

"God is angry at the suffering you've endured," I said. "God loves us all equally. When some take more than their share, leaving others, like you, scrounging in the streets, God gets upset. Your pain is eating away your spirit. Unless you find a constructive outlet, it will destroy you. Righteous anger at injustice is biblical."

Lencho didn't respond. But soon afterward he indicated that he would return to the group as long as he didn't have to say anything.

We went back to the class. "Lencho feels bad at having received a breakfast he didn't deserve," I said. I looked at the room full of poor peasants. "You didn't deserve to be born into poor Salvadoran families and I didn't deserve to be born into a rich North American family. Can you understand how bad I feel, knowing I received something I didn't deserve?"

Heads were nodding. The special breakfast had helped us break through some of the class and cultural barriers that separated us.

Earlier we had talked about the fact that the poor live close to and need each other. Their lives naturally mix and intertwine. The rich, on the other hand, isolate themselves, living independently behind walls and fences.

I reminded them that the four with the special breakfast wouldn't have felt bad if they had eaten apart because they would have assumed that everyone was eating the same food. "Many rich people don't even realize the misery of the poor because their lives never touch." Again, I sensed a break through in understanding each other.

But patterns which favor the rich and reinforce the victimization of the poor are hard to break. As we finished eating lunch that day, the cook, feeling terrible that I wasn't one of the four who had received a special breakfast that morning, offered me a second bowl of soup. I was the only one she approached.

As I turned the cook down, a group coordinator with whom I had been working closely for the last two years caught my eye. She had noted the interchange between the cook and me. She told me later that she now understood why I had refused to wear my new running shoes until she was able to replace her own worn-out rubber sandals.

Through the morning's discussion, God gave me insight into something I had been struggling with since our MCC discussions two weeks earlier.

I shared my thoughts with the promoters. "I don't have lots of money, at least compared to North Americans, but I do have resources, education, opportunities, security. It isn't fair for me to have so many more resources than you. I don't deserve them.

"But I have two choices. I can isolate myself from you so that I don't feel guilty. Or I can dedicate my resources to your benefit. I'm choosing to dedicate them to you."

And so I committed myself to cast my lot with the poor. This was a confirmation of the direction my life had been taking for some time.

Two weeks later I received another note telling me to call home as soon as possible. Since I was planning to go to San

Salvador the next day anyway, I quickly packed my bag and left that afternoon. The medical report was serious. Dad's condition was deteriorating rapidly, this time not from pneumonia or other secondary problems but from pressure on the brain.

I called again the following day. He was restless and in severe pain. My sister put the phone to his ear. I spoke to him and he responded with an enthusiastic jumble of unintelligible words. Later I learned that except for that brief period of recognition, he had been unresponsive all day. He was also able to rest afterward. It seemed he was able to relax once he knew I realized he was dying.

I bought my ticket to fly home the following day. I had no guarantee what I would find at home. In May Dad had been better than expected. It didn't seem likely, but maybe he would pull through again. It was hard to know how to prepare myself psychologically as I vacillated between not wanting him to die yet hoping his struggle would not be prolonged.

I had a short layover in Miami and called home to confirm my arrival time. It was then that I learned Dad had died at 9:50 the night before. Donna had been unable to get a call through to San Salvador. Isolated and alone in the busy airport, I tried to phone five or six different friends. But it was a Sunday afternoon in the summertime and no one was home. I sat fighting the tears. I knew what I was dealing with. But perhaps not knowing was preferable after all.

The next week was a blur of funeral plans, decisions, and people. I longed for solitude and was relieved that I could spend several weeks at the Loretto Motherhouse in Kentucky, the same place where I had made my retreat in October. I was glad for a peaceful environment where I could read and write. The idea of writing a book had been unexpectedly presented to me in January and I sensed that writing was to be part of my healing process.

Although it had occurred to me that the loss of a second parent would be different from losing the first, I was taken aback by the myriad of connecting losses. A chapter of my life had ended—the chapter where I was a daughter taken care of by my parents, where "home" was a specific place, where my father linked me to my siblings and to my home church.

The chapter that had ended had already been moving toward closure. But the transition is normally gradual. Roles switch as adult children begin caring for their aging parents. Time was already redefining my home in Springfield from the place where I always took for granted I belonged to the place I grew up. My sense of home was in transition when Dad got sick. So even as I grieved my loss, I wasn't sure if I was grieving a memory of what I used to have, an ideal of what I wished I had, or a concrete reality.

Those three weeks in Kentucky were renewing. I didn't feel my loss, however, until I returned to El Salvador. Being with friends who had walked with me through the months of waiting helped bring down the defenses guarding my emotions. Trying to return to "normal" life reminded me that something was terribly wrong.

I recognized my need to grieve. But the demanding responsibilities of work and the possibility of another military offensive kept my feelings checked. An October journal entry records my thoughts.

> It's two months ago today that Dad died. My emotions feel submerged although I think they could come to the surface if they had a chance. But where is the opportunity? Survival demands constantly moving forward. The present is all-consuming. It takes specific effort to create the space to grieve the past.

I wanted to learn whatever God had to teach me through my pain. Sadness was an overwhelmingly powerful emotion during that time. My own sadness made me more sensitive to the pain of others. I felt as if sadness was coursing through my life like a torrential rain, scarring and eroding my heart.

But if that was what God had for me, I wanted to embrace it. I'm glad for the friend who reminded me that, while it's true that we learn from pain and suffering, we also have a biblical right to stand against it. God wants joy and wholeness for us. We can claim that at the same time we embrace what we can learn from life experiences.

Feeling scattered and frazzled in November, I took two days off in San Salvador. I functioned well when busy but as soon as I stopped I felt exhausted and depressed. It wasn't surprising that November was difficult. Dad's surgery had been exactly a year earlier, both of my parent's birthdays were in early December, and holidays always bring back memories. The escalated military activity in November was also emotionally and physically exhausting. I realized I needed to take specific measures to cope with the stress.

14

Living the Contradictions

I went to the U.S. for a two-week vacation. Following my instinct, I returned to the Loretto Motherhouse in Kentucky. I had stayed there on two other occasions and knew it to be a place of prayer and quiet. Five months later I was still there writing this book.

January was particularly significant as I dealt with my impotence, anger, and sadness.

January 14, 1991

I arrived at Loretto Motherhouse on Sunday afternoon. Already I know that this is where I will be able to begin dealing honestly with the darkness. A wise friend readily understood what I was trying to express. She identified the element of anger which I hadn't thought about as such. I'm sure she is right about my need to get it out in the open.

It was frightening to allow myself to feel the darkness. I couldn't see. I didn't understand. I was reassured by Psalm 97:2 which describes God as surrounded by thick clouds and darkness. I had to be willing to enter the darkness in my search for God. Job inspired me as well. In chapter 23, he declares, "The Almighty has terrified me. Yet I am not silenced by the darkness, by the thick darkness that covers my face." Job didn't give in to his terror. I didn't have to either.

January 18, 1991
Tuesday morning I tried to put my finger on the anger, which was nebulous and vague. I was in the woods by the pond thinking about fear. I wasn't scared to die when I was caught in the attack on November 20. But I was scared of dying needlessly. I didn't want my death to be ineffective. Then it struck me. My anger was at my own impotence.

I felt impotent and powerless in the face of pain and death. I snapped little twigs as the tears of frustration began to flow. But the twigs weren't enough. I picked up a branch and hit it against the ground. Then I found another one and smashed it against a tree trunk, and another and another. It was a perfect outlet for my rage. I was taken aback by the strength of my feelings. I kept thinking that I can work my fingers to the bone and even give up my life but it will never be enough.

During the days that followed I thought about Jesus and the impotence he must have felt on the cross. How could I move through the darkness, anger, and fear to the other side, where impotence gives birth to God's power?

Once my anger had subsided, I was filled with sadness.

January 18, 1991
I woke up yesterday feeling sad. There is so much sadness in our world and now we're at war in the Persian Gulf. I think God must feel sad as well.
A friend made an important distinction between sadness and depression. She said that Christians sensitive to God's pain at the human condition will feel sadness. Normally we can carry sadness without being overpowered by it. Depression occurs if the sadness becomes so great that it overwhelms us.

It struck me that while anger needs to be transformed into creative energy, sadness needs to be befriended. Sadness I will always carry with me to a certain extent. I need to open the constricted channels of my heart so it can flow through me to the heart of God.

Impotence was a common thread as I thought about anger, compassion, and waiting. I would get angry at the helplessness which prevented me from compassionately accompanying people in their pain. It was easier to withdraw. Waiting had negative connotations as well. I identified waiting with doing nothing.

January 21, 1991

Waiting is hard. It was almost a relief when war broke out in the Middle East because the uncertainty was finally over. The inevitable had happened. How much destruction have we done simply because anything was better than "helplessly" waiting?

But God calls us to wait. Waiting on God implies rest and strength. "It is good to wait quietly for the salvation of the Lord."

My last few months in El Salvador I had been hit with injustice, violence, and pain. Feeling the reality of evil, I couldn't maintain a naive outlook on life.

January 23, 1991

With all naiveté gone, how can I still embrace life as good and God-given? How can I know that evil exists and still be shocked by it?

I'm reminded of Cathy's car. I borrowed it, expecting it wouldn't start in the morning, so when it did I was pleasantly surprised. I thought maybe I should treat life that way, be prepared for the bad and surprised at the good. But that isn't what I want. I want to expect that life is good because that's how God intends for it to be.

I guess what I'm saying is that I want to risk hope—not

with the naive assumption that life should be easy, but as a conscious choice to be shocked by the evil that I know exists.

As I got in touch with my grief, I realized that I wasn't only grieving my father's death but also my powerlessness and loss of innocence.

January 26, 1991

Grief includes the disappointments, times of feeling helpless, self-doubt, insecurity, separation. I grieve that I'm not who I wish I were. I disappoint myself when I don't live up to my expectations. I want so much to do what's right, to do what would be most helpful, to get to the root of the problems and not just apply superficial Band-Aids.

It was hard to be patient and allow myself the time I needed. Once I have an insight into a problem, I tend to think it should be solved. I felt guilty for the luxury of reflective time and space.

January 28, 1991

There's so much work to be done. How can I justify reflective time when there are others who need it more than I do? It's hard to be gentle with myself.

Here I am at Loretto Motherhouse, an environment steeped with the warmth of maturity and prayer. Why am I privileged to be here? Intellectually and theologically, I tell myself that it is a gift of God's grace that I can't explain. I can only accept it with a grateful heart. I thought I was doing that until the other day, when Susan gently and tenderly massaged the knots in my back and neck.

When she left I cried for several hours. Why was it so difficult to receive warmth and caring? I was painfully aware that I can't be gentle with others if I'm not gentle with myself. And that when I do violence to myself I do violence to others.

As I dealt with my emotions, the physical tightness I had been feeling in my chest became more pronounced, or at least more obvious. It reminded me of sitting in the hospital waiting for the surgeon after Dad's operation. The doctor finally walked in and I knew that in a minute the waiting would be over. My heart was steeled, prepared for anything.

January 29, 1991

I've been trying to unsteel my heart. The barriers went up to protect myself, to keep the pain out of the vulnerable center of my being. Ironically, though, the very act of self-protection is now smothering me. The armor needs to be dismantled.

As I let go of the armor crushing my heart and sink deep into the darkness, I realize there is another, deeper reality. I begin to sense not a bright light, but an illuminating glow. A warmth like the dawn, waiting in hope to transform the night. Then I know that even the darkness is encompassed by tenderness and mercy.

When I treat myself with the same gentleness and compassion with which God treats our world, I in a small way encompass the darkness of my failures, pain, doubts, and insecurities. They don't disappear but their boundaries are defined by gentleness. Within the boundaries of my own darkness there is room for the pain, doubt, and fear of others.

January 30, 1991

This morning I pictured a vise grip, the red one screwed to the table in Dad's workshop. I felt my heart squeezed between the metal teeth. But then the vise was replaced by gentle hands, hands that provide security and support without squeezing. They give as my heart expands, allowing room for growth. I pictured the vise grip loosening and the constricting bands melting, conquered not by strength but surrender.

The months in Kentucky passed quickly as I wrote and enjoyed the company of the sisters. The gradual signs of winter passing into spring reflected the awakening I felt in my heart and soul.

My time of concentrated writing and reflection was ending. My last Sunday afternoon I sat in the woods by the lake enjoying the quiet peacefulness and writing in my journal. "It took several months to relax," I wrote. "I wonder how long I will feel this way once I return to El Salvador."

Finishing the sentence, I looked up and saw a full rainbow so clear and bright the lake reflected it. I felt reassured as I thought of the rainbow as a symbol of hope and promise. The tears and darkness are not eliminated, but light reflecting off the tears produces a kaleidoscope of color.

I returned to El Salvador at the beginning of June. I was concerned about going back. Would I lose perspective again? Would I be gentle with myself and others in the midst of the harsh reality of war and oppression? Five months later I'm celebrating the fact that the healing process has continued.

November 23, 1991

Yesterday my mind wandered as I traveled. I felt content and relaxed. Suddenly it struck me. How long has it been since I've felt so good? Last November I was dealing with my father's recent death and the escalated military activity. The November before that I had just backed out of my speaking commitments due to emotional and physical exhaustion when I learned Dad had a brain tumor. At least two years have passed since I've felt genuinely relaxed and healthy!

I realized I couldn't identify exactly when the darkness started or when it ended. But has it ended? Maybe my perception has changed. A year ago the darkness filled me with desperation. I felt overwhelmed and smothered by heaviness. Now I sense the positive aspects of darkness. I think of a seed buried in the blackness of mother earth, its tender roots stretching downward for nurture and strength. I think of the darkness of night and rest. I think of the silent blackness of a mother's womb as new life takes form. I feel reassured. Both aspects of the darkness are real. I'm struck by the contradiction.

The thread of contradictions weaves its way throughout my experiences in Latin America. I've struggled with being a North American, Mennonite pacifist with the security of education and support, working with the poor in war-torn El Salvador among the Catholics.

At times, I've wished I could live in one world or the other instead of having to bridge what seems to be two different worlds. But as I recognize the contradictions and work at integrating my experiences, I realize that the dichotomies and distinctions dividing "my world in El Salvador" from "my world in the United States" are false. I'm actually being stretched between the poles of one world created whole by God, yet cut and divided by human beings as we compete for power and control.

Parker J. Palmer writes, "Boldly become a pole of opposition; live the contradiction. The false crosses will fall away, while those we must accept will stay there in the middle of our lives, pulling right and left, up and down, until they pull us open at our true center, a center where we are one with God, a center which we find only on the way of the cross."[22]

Living out the contradictions is painful. I would rather resolve them by living in the middle. I want to fill the hole that forms as I'm stretched between the poles, not leave it empty. But the center belongs to God. It is a holy space in the depth of my soul where God can dwell.

In his book *A Spirituality of Hope*, Segundo Galilea writes, "Christian hope . . . is the difference between life as absurd and life as mystery."[23]

Vultures and butterflies, good and evil, life and death. Living the poles of contradiction is a life-giving mystery.

Notes

1. Mary Jo Leddy, *Reweaving Religious Life* (Mystic, Conn.: Twenty-Third Publications, 1991), p. 126.

2. LTC A. J. Bacevich, LTC James De Hallums, LTC Richard H. White, LTC Thomas F. Young, "American Military Policy in Small Wars: The Case of El Salvador," March 1988, p. 3.

3. Ibid. p. 13.

4. Alfonso Chardy, "U.S. will use Central America to test 'violent peace' doctrine," *Miami Herald*, October 1, 1986.

5. Jack Nelson-Pallmeyer, *War Against the Poor, Low-Intensity Conflict and Christian Faith* (Maryknoll, N.Y.: Orbis Books, 1989), p. 31.

6. John Howard Yoder, *The Politics of Jesus* (Eerdmans, 1979), p. 150.

7. Thomas Merton, *New Seeds of Contemplation* (Norfolk, Conn.: New Directions, 1961), p. 151.

8. Ibid. p. 14.

9. Ibid. p. 72

10. Ibid. p. 47.

11. Anthony de Mello, *The Song of the Bird* (Garden City, N.J.: Image Books, 1982), p. 8.

12. Tom Barry, *El Salvador Country Guide* (Albuquerque,

NM.: The Inter-Hemispheric Education Resource Center, 1990), p. 109.

13. Thomas Merton, *New Seeds of Contemplation*, p. 71

14. Albert Nolan, *God in South Africa* (Grand Rapids: Eerdmans, 1988), 67.

15. Arturo Paoli, *Gather Together in My Name* (Maryknoll, NY.: Orbis Books, 1987), p. 60.

16. John Howard Yoder, *Politics of Jesus*, p. 146.

17. Albert Nolan, "Taking Sides," Special issue 2, year 3, p. 10.

18. Albert Nolan, *God in South Africa* (Grand Rapids: Eerdmans, 1988), p. 104.

19. Jurgen Moltmann, *Experiences of God* (Philadelphia: Fortress Press, 1980), p. 19.

20. Dorothee Soelle, *To Work and to Love: A Theology of Creation* (Philadelphia: Fortress Press, 1984), p. 161.

21. Interview with Jon Sobrino, "The Greatest Love," *Sojourners Magazine*, April 1990.

22. Parker J. Palmer, "The Way of the Cross," *Weavings*, March/April 1991, p. 20.

23. Segundo Galilea, *A Spirituality of Hope* (Maryknoll, N.Y.: Orbis, 1988), p. 17.

The Author

Susan Classen was born in Springfield, Ohio. She was the youngest of three girls, raised in the warmth of a stable, nurturing home. Her parents' commitment to active church involvement strongly influenced her childhood.

She attended Eastern Mennonite College 1975-1979, and earned a degree in nursing. After graduation, Susan worked in a hospital for a year, then accepted an assignment with the Mennonite Central Committee in Bolivia. She lived in an isolated Bolivian village for two years before moving to El Salvador in 1984.

Eight years later, Susan continues to find El Salvador a demanding yet rewarding place to live. Her health work provides a variety of opportunities to identify with people whose lives have been disrupted by poverty, oppression, and war.

Susan is a member of the Support Circle, a community of sixteen single Mennonite women committed to supporting each other in their work with the poor.